REMEMBER WHO YOU ARE

THE GREATEST AFRICAN TRIBE

By David Lloyd.

TABLE OF CONTENTS

ACKNOWLEDGMENTS

In loving memory of David P Lloyd Sr. &
King Mambali

Dedicated to
Community Scholars of the 6-Pages-A-Day
Urban Reading Club.

Special thanks to

Shanika Ofori
www.democracynow.org
www.history.com
www.cnn.com

INTRODUCTION

"Remember Who You Are" is the profound awakening of African-American intellectuals as a collective African tribe.

The message centers on African-Americans taking pride in their many cultural and political achievements as arguably *"the most influential culture the world has ever seen"*. The author, originally from Africa, expounds on the extraordinary culture, appropriately labeling African Americans as **"The Greatest African Tribe"** based off their African ancestral roots and astonishing accomplishments in spite of numerous racial challenges.

It presents a forward thinking hundred year vision, advocating for economic freedom rooted in support of black owned businesses in the United States and Africa.

It stresses that the respect of African descendants all around the world is directly linked to economics and African continental perception. It campaigns for **"absolute respect"** achieved through self-love and economic empowerment as being the only true remedy for racial suffering.

It also lists non-physical reasons to be proud of

being born black. Something many people struggle articulating. The author reminds African-Americans that they are arguably the strongest African bloodline as they are a result of an unnatural selection process of the last 500 years in which only the strongest of strongest survived. He calls for African-Americans to take a real interest in Africa, demonstrating that other nations such as China, are building wealth in Africa while African-Americans are self-alienating from their homeland. He gives different examples of the possibilities of economic emancipation as a result of doing business with Africa. He challenges African-Americans and Africans to not only look to the glory days of ancient African kingdoms for cultural pride but instead have a plan for the next 100 years. He insists the plan must involve extensive deliberate coordination between African-American communities and African communities.

The book begins with the author describing a dream he had of his deceased grandfather who told him to "Remember who he was." The author describes struggling with his identity as he tried to interpret the meaning of the dream. He finally discovers the true meaning of the dream months later, during a conversation with a friend. He realized the dream wasn't just for him to remember who he was, but it was a call for an entire generation of African-Americans to remember who they were. The author being originally from Africa himself describes what it was like growing up in Africa. He also describes his transition to the United States and the challenges he faced with racism.

LEGACY

noun leg·a·cy \ ˈle-gə-sē \
Something transmitted by or received from
an ancestor or predecessor or from the past.

What will be your legacy? What identity will your descendants inherit?

Will you continue the tradition of laying the foundation for a better, brighter future as did your ancestors, or will you fail to live up to your full potential?

Africans and African-Americans alike must answer these questions. I believe it's the duty of our generation to accomplish what is yet to be achieved – **Absolute respect**.

In order to solve a problem one must first identify what to solve for. Just as you tried to solve for "X" in your algebra class; we need to solve for our "X".

So when we say "Black Lives Matter", what are we trying to solve for?

Are we trying to change racist minds to empathize with our plight?

Are we trying to rid the world of racism?

Can we truly rid the world of racism?

I think energy spent on trying to change every racist soul into a Bernie Sanders is energy misplaced. I believe the "X" we seek is **Respect**. Respect will make

Black lives matter.

Respect from those in positions of power. Those who have the ability to impact our livelihood. We cannot rid the world of racism until we overcome the disrespect of the ruling class.

Every problem related to racism, starting from before slavery and onwards has occurred because those in power do not respect Africans – "Blacks".

Our path to global-respect starts with self-respect and the realization of self-power. Self-respect starts with **knowing who we are and loving ourselves**. Beginning with absolute acceptance of African-Americans as an extension Africa. It's time to blur the line between the two.

However, we must preserve African-American identity as it exists today. Let those who wish to identify exclusively with their African ancestral tribe do so, but let's not forget to empower authentic African-American culture in the process. African-American culture is perfect just as it is. It should continue to evolve organically. I believe it is essential that we recognize its brilliance and depth as an important part of Africa's legacy. Just as we recognize the brilliance and depth of all three thousand African tribes. African-Americans are a congregation of African descendants. For this reason I believe it is appropriate to categorize the group as an African tribe.

Many other diaspora tribes exist in Haiti, Brazil, Britain, Jamaica, etc. But for purposes of this discussion, I will focus on one I believe to be the greatest – The African-American tribe. African-Americans and Africa need to unite as one force.

Here's why – Think about the subject of reparations. African-Americans suffered the torments of slavery for hundreds of years. Literally building the United States into the world's premiere super power. However, to this day, they have not received any compensation for reparations. Why is that?

On the other hand, according to a February 1999 article on democracynow.org, the Justice Department closed the books on a $1.6 billion reparations program for ethnic Japanese interned in American camps during World War II, and settled with 181 ethnic Japanese from Latin America who suffered similar treatment. The redress program made $20,000 payments to 82,210 Japanese Americans or their heirs. Under a federal court settlement the balance of the fund was left over to make $5,000 payments to Latin American Japanese.

So why weren't the same considerations given to African-Americans? After all, African Americans were in bondage longer and contributed more free labor to the United States than any other ethnic group. As Angela Rye says, "We built this joint".

Could it be because no foreign government with serious American interests advocated for African-Americans? I believe this could be one major contributing factor.

In both America and Germany (pertaining to the Jews) reparations were paid in consideration of diplomatic influence of foreign governments. The US needed to establish relations with Japan, a now major strategic ally. Germany needed to establish relations with Israel, now a major Middle Eastern ally.

What foreign nation advocates for the plight of African-Americans? I believe herein lies one reason why there needs to be strong relations between pro-American, African countries and African-Americans. The African-American tribe should leverage international support as a tool.

I must point out that no one is at fault for the lack of international relationships. There simply wasn't any real opportunity for meaningful coordination. African-Americans were dealing with the challenges of slavery, Jim Crow and segregation, whilst Africans were dealing with colonization.

Thanks to efforts of previous generations in America and Africa, our generation has the opportunity to build the necessary relationships – this is our legacy. We must come up with holistic solutions to holistic problems.

The second step in gaining respect is acquiring power. Now I know some may immediately think "Black Liberation Army", but that school of thought is outdated. Frankly any army of sorts will not garner respect, not even fear, just another reason to demonize efforts. The goal is to be respected. I cannot stress this enough. Such actions will simply cause an endless loop of provocation. We're smarter than that.

Understand that power structures of the world have changed. First there was the church, then governments, and now its corporations. One doesn't need an army nor violence to effect change, one needs a corporation. African-Americans need to think like and become a corporation. Like all corporations, you need an international foot print – again, herein comes

Africa.

If you want to know what matters to a person, observe what they choose to spend their money on. Likewise, if you want to know what matters to the United States government, observe what it spends tax payer money on. US government officials are indebted to those who bank roll elections. Many times the interests of these puppet masters are overseas. African-Americans could leverage African leaders to accomplish common goals. Hypothetically, if Exxon Mobile was on the verge of acquiring a lucrative oil contract in Angola, during the Flint Michigan water crisis. If a good enough relationship existed, African-American leaders could've potentially asked the Angolan government to catalyze a resolution. Even though the two situations are a world away and not even remotely related, Exxon Mobile has significant influence on Capitol Hill. Flint would've received the congressional attention it deserved. Unfortunately, probably not entirely in the interest of Flint, but in the interest of Exxon Mobile. Regardless a goal would've been accomplished.

I understand that this hypothetical scenario of leveraging African power is reserved for African-American tribe leaders – whoever they may be. However, there are other ways the average tribe member can exercise their power – through votes and financial contributions.

Lately there's been an out pouring of support for African-American business. A great initiative! I highly encourage it. It's precisely what this book is about. However, some may be under the assumption that supporting African-American businesses is an effective way of advocating for policy change. This simply isn't true. If our goal is policy change, then we need to directly influence those in the legislature. We need votes and campaign funding to effect change. Attempting to keep money out of the "system" and in African-American communities is a myth. The system doesn't lose a penny – it still collects taxes from African-American businesses.

A better approach is for the tribe to become a corporation and form a Super PAC (Political Action Committee). We need to borrow a page from the Jewish playbook and have an organization of paid lobbyists. We shouldn't look to the outside for help, otherwise we risk being indebted to competing interests. Instead we need to self-fund with simple fundraising initiatives such as monthly membership dues.

Protesting in the streets is great for media attention, but it simply doesn't go far enough. We can do better. We have the finances and intellectual talent to garner legislative respect. Frankly, I don't care if someone chooses to hate me because of the color of my skin, as long as they're powerless to impact my livelihood. This is why we need to own the legislature. We simply need to think and function as one.

Take a look at an organization such as the NRA (National Rifle Association), they never as much as have a protest, yet they're probably the most influential organization on Capitol Hill. This is because they have the ability to make or break campaigns using financial contributions and member votes. This is what it takes to be respected.

THE MESSAGE

In the summer of 2016, I had a dream. This dream would haunt my thoughts like the ghost of Christmas past – it, was a message from my ancestor. The message was simply "Remember who you are." I struggled trying to 'remember' exactly who I was.

I wrote down pages of my memories, my life, and my family history. I consulted with family and friends, asking them "who am I?" But no matter how deep I searched, I couldn't get rid of the feeling that something was missing.

It wasn't until I asked the question of someone else did I realize what I felt was the true meaning of the dream. This message wasn't for me alone, but was for me to share with every American of African descent willing to receive it.

The dream was a calling to the Greatest African Tribe.

I dreamt of my grandfather - my deceased grandfather that is. It was puzzling. I immediately knew that this was no ordinary dream because I seldom spent time with my grandfather; and for no other reason than, we lived in different cities and most recently, on different continents. I visited him a couple of times during school holidays. Other than that, I mainly saw him on 'special' occasions - weddings or funerals.

My grandfather passed in 2005, long after I moved to the United States, from Africa. I wondered how I could have a dream about him ten years later. I woke up from my dream, sat up in my bed and just thought "what the hell was that about?!"

The dream was very vivid. I was walking down a path on a dirt road. To my left, was a tree that towered approximately six stories high. The base of its trunk was as wide as two cars laid next to each other. Its branches were short and covered with a thicket of dark green leaves, almost resembling a bush of broccoli. Its bark was an orange-red color, reminding me of a beautiful sunset. The tree grew right where there was a bend in the road.

The dirt road was sand and gravel, almost like a dessert. I felt the sand break as I walked through it. It felt like walking through sand at a beach. I felt the wind blowing across my face - a slight breeze. I thought to myself "This is one very lucid dream." I was fully aware I was dreaming. Something I rarely experience. I decided to go exploring – something I always try to do whenever I have these rare dreams. I try to walk around, noting every aspect of the dream. Especially, if I am dreaming of a place that I do not recognize.

I walked down the road to see where it led. I walked around the bend, slightly passed the big tree to my left. I heard a man's voice. It was soft and calm, and he said "shangwe, shangwe" – a greeting I was familiar with

(This is how elders on my mother's side of the family would greet. I believe its direct translation is 'Welcome.' It is used in place of 'Hello.')

I turned to look back in the direction of the voice. Standing behind me, was my grandfather. Being aware that I was in a dream and fully aware he was deceased, I said, "Shanene (meaning grandfather), I can't wait to tell mom that I saw you in my dream!" He laughed and just said, "Remember who you are." I was puzzled. I asked him what he meant. But he just repeated himself saying "remember who you are." He then smiled and disappeared.

I woke up puzzled but happy. I felt as though I had received the greatest hint to my life's purpose. Except, it was hidden deep in the history of who I was, and all I needed to do was 'remember.' I called my mother to tell her about my dream. I could hear the skepticism in her voice. But being a religious person, she left me with one bit of advice almost all church going black mothers say – pray about it.

Days past and I couldn't find a satisfactory answer to the question "Who am I?" Every time I believed I had found the answer, there would be another layer to peel away.

"Can I truly identify myself?"

"Who do I know who can truly identify themselves?"

These are questions I asked myself. Oddly enough, as silly as it may be, the first hint of how I should be able to identify myself, came to me as I was watching an episode of Game of Thrones. In it, the fictional character, 'Khaleesi' identifies herself in the most elaborate way. If you've watched Game of Thrones, then you'd know who exactly I'm referring to. If you have not, you should - it's a great show!

Khaleesi identifies herself as

"Daenerys Stormborn of the House Targaryen, First of her name, the Unburnt, Queen of Meereen, Queen of the Andals, the Rhoynar and the First Men, Khaleesi of the Great Grass Sea, Breaker of Chains and Mother of Dragons, protector of the realm and ruler of the seven kingdoms."

I thought to myself, "Here is someone who knows who exactly she is." So using the only example I had of what I thought was a great description in identity – Khaleesi; I tried to identify exactly who I was.

I started with the basics. Who are my parents? Who are my grandparents? Where did they come from? Where was I born? What's my culture? Who are my people? My name, where did my name come from? Etc. I wrote down everything I knew about myself. It was a lot. But I still felt something was missing. I felt that I still hadn't found what my ancestor was trying to tell me.

I shared my dream and what I learned about myself with a friend. We laughed about it. We tried to brainstorm what else it may be that I was missing. We peeled the layers all the way back until there was nothing earthly left to identify me by. So we just said "spirit! – you're a spirit!"

At first, I thought Spirit was it, but I still had this feeling inside telling me that wasn't the meaning of the dream. Frustrated with not being able to answer the question for myself, I asked my friend if she had ever thought about who she was.

There were several pauses and moments of deep thought as she tried to go down the list. Naming parents, grandparents, place of birth, etc. But when I asked about tribe and culture she simply said *"You're lucky that you're first generation African American. You know exactly where you came from, who your people are, and what your culture is".* There was a disappointment and a familiar sadness in her voice. I didn't know how to respond besides "Yea, I guess so."

I understood her pain and her longing for African identity. I empathized with the challenges her ancestors (my "American" grandparents) went through.

But oddly enough, I saw more than just challenges; I saw victories.

I couldn't agree with the statement that she didn't have a tribe or culture; though I know, she meant it in the context of "African culture" and "African Tribe." Though that which is born of Africans is "African." One must REMEMBER that African-Americans, are really just Africans born in America. So everything "African-American" really is "African." With that, we can definitely conclude that African-American culture is African culture.

See, Africa is one – Africans are one. Early Europeans divided Africa and Africans both regionally and mentally. This is why I refer to the Africans who went through slavery as my Kin. Those were my grandparents too.

We must all REMEMBER that families were split

during slavery. It's 100% true that today there are African-Americans living in the US, who are blood relatives of Africans on the continent – as they share a common great, great grandfather/grandmother. Think about that. I don't think we take enough time to stop and ponder that.

Time and history have drawn a distinction between "African-American" and "African," but in reality, we're talking about the same family, just in different parts of the world. With experiences unique to their location. No different than my family today. My mother and sisters are in Africa, while I'm here in America. If I were never to return to Africa, my great, great grandchildren would still be African and kin, to my sister's great, great grandchildren.

So let me make one thing abundantly clear – African-Americans do not need anyone's permission to claim Africa. It has been, and always will be their motherland.

Another to REMEMBER is that no African family would have sold their family member into slavery. Africans were kidnapped and sold by Arabs and Europeans. But also, by other Africans who weren't their kin. There were some Africans that were corrupted by greed and wealth who participated in the trade of human beings. As in any society, there is always a fringe criminal element that dishonors its heritage.

We also know that history is greatly Eurocentric. Meaning it's written in a way that favors the European narrative. This narrative would like to tell us that mainstream Africans and not just the criminal element, sold other Africans into slavery. I just don't believe it.

Here's why – The older generation of Africans were a collective society versus the western individualistic society. Meaning family and community were more important than wealth.

A question to ask yourself is, why would mainstream Africans sell their fellow African to Europeans supposedly for wealth gain when there was already abundant wealth in Africa? Think about it. The African ruling class was already wealthy.

Gold, Silver, Diamonds, Land, virtually every possible concept of wealth was already in Africa. Matter of fact, Europeans came to Africa looking for these very same resources. So what could they have possibly brought to trade with the African ruling class that would have been so valuable that they would sell their own people?

I believe the truth is, Europeans came with a divide-and-conquer agenda. They had weapons that Africans simply weren't prepared for. One of which was psychological warfare. They set up colonies and economies. They then began the systemic process of plundering resources. While pitting one African tribe against another. Supporting which ever tribe served their interest. How do I know this? – Because it's still going on today! Many smaller African clans fell victim to these proxy wars and kidnapping raids. These Africans were then transported to the Americas.

This book is a message to the descendants of those Africans. Reminding them that Africa has not forgotten them. Africa is proud of them. For despite their trials and tribulations, they have still become the

Greatest African Tribe the world has ever seen.

Now you may wonder why I keep referring to African-Americans as a "Tribe." Why is this label important? It's important because it REMINDS the African-American community that they are indeed an extension of Africa. Africa has many tribes which developed in some of the same ways the African-American community developed - people of similar backgrounds and experience coming together.

Let's walk through the official definition of a tribe and compare it to the African-American situation. By definition, a tribe is – "*a social division in a traditional society consisting of families or communities linked by social, economic, religious, or blood ties, with a common culture and dialect, typically having a recognized leader.*" Now compare that to the African-American situation - Every African-American is descendant from Africa. Every African-American, shares similar social, economic ties with a common culture and dialect.

As for the part of the definition mentioning a "recognized leader." I believe that is yet to come. There have been several leaders over the centuries, maybe most notably Martin Luther King, but I believe a time is coming when another leader will emerge. A leader who will lead the tribe to economic freedom – real freedom.

See, you can change the name, change the language, even change the thought process, but Africa has a way of stamping its people. Melanin-full skin is something you just can't quite get rid of. It stays as a constant reminder, as though saying "if found, return to Africa." Hence, we know for sure that every black person, whether they agree with it or not belong to Africa. This is why it is important to appropriately label African-Americans, not just as a community, but as an African tribe.

My ultimate point is that there should not be a distinction in unity between African Americans and Africans. We were separated for 400-500 years – but we're here now. Thanks to technological advances we can now communicate with one another. The African-American tribe can now communicate with their Kin in Africa. They can now see the motherland for themselves through their own eyes, or through images that have been captured by Africans themselves and not the dishonest media. Likewise, all the tribes of Africa can learn a great deal from the African-American tribe. There's a lot they can teach about how to do more with less. Keep in mind; these are people who rose from slavery to the White House.

WHERE DID
WE GO WRONG?

Where did we go wrong?" on the colonization of Africa, is a question that every person of African ancestry has asked themselves at one point or another - or at least should ask. The responses to this question vary greatly from "African incompetence" to "European devils..." to even "Gods will."

Regardless of how you answer this question, 'historical facts', if not divine intervention, are probably at the center of your response.

Winston Churchill former British Prime Minister and the man who led Great Britain during the Second World War once said "history is written by the victor." No other words couldn't be truer.

Lately, I've been bombarded with the realization that we live in a world of "alternative facts." The 'truth' is now relative - or maybe it has always been?

Thanks to competing media sources, we see it more plainly.

It's both humorous and scary to be able to flip from one news channel to the next and witness entirely different narratives of what the 'truth' is. Left-leaning media spins a news story to a leftist agenda, and right-leaning media spins it in the opposite direction.

So who can you trust?

We too are to blame as we are more inclined to receive our information from sources that agree with our biases.

Sometimes we may not even have a bias, but because we simply do not have enough information to form an opinion, we assume what we're being told is true because it's coming from a 'credible' source. For example, most people I've met in the U.S sincerely believe that Africa is rampant with wars, starvation, and crime – that couldn't be further from the truth. Such a narrowly focused narrative is no different than a person reporting on what may be going on in the south side of Chicago and using it as an account for the daily life of all black people in America.

With that said, I can only imagine how history has been conveniently edited for the benefit of competing agendas.

I've become extremely skeptical in relying on historical 'facts' about the colonization of Africa and slavery in Africa. Earlier on as I began to write this, I thought about including several pieces of historical facts to make my case, but then I thought it hypocritical because even as I read through the facts, I couldn't help but wonder how they've been edited.

I think it best to not look at history so blindly as though the writers had no bias or no naivety.

While we have respect for honest historians and the

entire field of study, we must be open to the possibility that some information that's been passed down, even to them, could be lies.

Keep in mind, the world being flat was once a historical "fact". Africans being intellectually inferior to Europeans was once a historical "fact". I could fill out several books with just the debunked historical lies and assumptions and propaganda made over the centuries. So to you the reader, I ask that you keep this in mind when you think about what you think you know as fact about Africa.

Let's start with what opposing sides can agree as being true today.

1. Africa is a large continent with various resources.
2. For centuries, Europe has had a great interest in Africa.
3. The great pyramids of Egypt were constructed as early as 2600 BC (maybe even before that) proving that civilization began in Africa.

That's as far as I'll go with historical facts.

So what happened? How did Africa start out as this great civilization and essentially fall from grace?

I believe the answer lies in the error of the premise of the question. Africa didn't fall from grace. Africa is still as graceful as ever, and some parts are as advanced as the rest of the world. I think the main difference is a difference in priorities and motivations. At some point, Africans stopped being primarily motivated by material wealth.

It's fair to say that Africans are not imperialistic.

That is - they're not interested in 'conquering' the world – a major motivator in technological advances. African governments don't have an interest in walking on the moon or a mission to Mars. They care about the day to day lives of their people. The ultimate aspirations of African people are mainly spiritual and not physical. Speak about religion and the supernatural world, and there you will find the motivations of the average African. One could argue pros and cons of their world view.

My assumption based on my experience with the older generation of Africans is this - for the most part, older generations were not motivated by material wealth. What some may see as a lack of ingenuity, really was a lack of motivation to create and acquire more 'stuff.' They were satisfied with their way of life. No different than an American hippie who finds no added pleasure in owning the newest model vehicle. Industry, innovation and modern wealth just wasn't something greatly valued. Africa had its own definition of wealth. Wealth was defined by family, respect, and honor. A man with a large well-respected family was admired. Material possessions were a matter of necessity and not necessarily flamboyance. A large herd of cattle, vast areas of land, were all necessary for the survival of the clan.

Now, of course, like with all things, there were exceptions. It's very important to distinguish between the values and lifestyles of the average African, from the values and lifestyles of African royalty. Using the remnants of a very small population of African royalty, such as Mansa Musa – the richest person in history, as an indicator of Africa's overall grandeur is as naïve as using Bill Gates as an indicator of achievement of the average American. The top 1% of any society should never be used as an indicator of the lifestyles and beliefs of the majority. The greater majority of the African continent simply didn't have a desire for grandeur. How do I know this? Because the African continent has enough resources to put on the grandest show the world has ever seen. But for thousands of years, the majority of the population really haven't cared to exploit these material resources – that is until the Europeans arrived. Even today, the older generation, my grandfather's generation, don't care much about material wealth as we understand it. However, my westernized generation has high regard for material wealth.

I believe it is precisely these values that the older generations had that made colonization possible. It's easier for someone to take something from you if you do not understand its true value or rather if you value something else in its place.

Europeans came from a land where the resources found in Africa were either non-existent or scarce, so they immediately had an appreciation of African resources. So they took advantage of the situation. Some of the natives resisted the occupation, but the resistance was not that as potent as, say, the Haitian revolution. Instead, some Africans decided to trade with the Europeans, often trading that of great value for that of little value. It was only after the Europeans had settled in and started treating Africans as second-class citizens in their own land, did the Africans realize the game the Europeans had played, and thus there were several African revolutions in opposition of colonization.

I believe Europeans took advantage of the humbleness and trustworthiness of Africans. This was brilliantly characterized in the novel "The Old Man and The Medal" a 1956 post-colonial novel by Cameroonian diplomat Ferdinand Oyono. In it, the main character "Meka" a native of a certain village under colonial rule, is to be given a Medal by the colonial masters for his cooperation. Meka had no idea what a Medal was. Meka gave up his land for the building of a church, he also gave his two sons to serve in the military to fight the Whiteman's war, where they both got killed. For his great contribution and sacrifice, the colonial masters rewarded Meka with a Medal. They told him it was the highest honor one could receive. This made an instant celebrity out of him. The whole village came out to see this thing called "Medal". They waited in awe to see what could be so valuable to the Whiteman that it could only be earned by one who had given up his land and sons. The euphoria was short-lived when the Whiteman pinned a little piece of metal on Meka's chest and thanked him for his sacrifice. That little piece of metal was the "Medal." The moral of the story was - be careful of the cunningness of the Whiteman. Meka gave the Whiteman everything he had, trusting in the 'good nature' of the Whiteman for an equally valuable reward. But in return all the Whiteman gave him was a small worthless piece of metal.

On a side note, remember this story when you think of the plight of the African-American tribe whose ancestors worked for free to build the world's super power and yet the most they've received in return is affirmative action.

To this day in some places in Africa, village chiefs are giving away large sloths of land for a fraction of the land's true value. Mines and mining contracts are being given to foreign investors pretty much for free with only "Medals" in return. I can only imagine what promises Europeans made in the days before colonization.

I'm not ashamed to say that my default setting is to blame Europe for all that's wrong with Africa, but I can't help but notice that Europe only does to Africa what Africa allows. Colonization ended when Africans decided enough was enough.

Likewise, the plunder of African resources will also stop when Africans decide to combat corruption and sincerely advocate for what's in the best interest of the poor. This can only occur with the right leadership. Unfortunately, too often we've seen African leaders who are easily corrupted by greed and power. Africans need to select leaders who are motivated by the success of their countries and the overall continent rather than their own personal gain. Otherwise, outside influences will continue to siphon resources. This is where I believe the influence of the African-American tribe would be most valuable. As the African-American tribe is in a better position to support African leaders without retribution from the opposition. The African-American tribe can use the American machine to change the game entirely. All it takes is an endorsement of African leaders who put the livelihood of their people ahead of their personal gain. One doesn't need to travel to Africa to be influential. Something as simple as Facebook campaigns, GoFundMe fundraisers or letters to the U.S congress in support of an African leader, would make a world of difference.

We can call ourselves "Kings" and "Queens" all day, but as long as the Kingdom isn't living up to its full potential, the rest of the world isn't going to respect us.

WE CAN BE FAIR

I n all fairness, not everything Europe did to Africa has turned out to be negative. There were some positive byproducts that resulted as a consequence of colonization.

In Zambia and Zimbabwe for example, most of the country's current infrastructure was built in colonial days.

The very fact that English is the national language in Zambia, has muted any tribal conflict that could have resulted from the mere appearance of one tribe being regarded as worthy of being the arbiters of the national language.

The tourism industry that many African countries rely heavily on has been compromised mainly of visitors from Europe.

Most importantly, many descendants of the colonial rulers still reside in Africa and have great love and appreciation for the continent. Conservation efforts of both African ethnic traditions and wildlife have been spearheaded by Europeans.

In some cases, the largest most productive farms that essentially feed the continent have been managed by the descendants of colonial rule. President Robert

Mugabe of Zimbabwe allegedly made the mistake of expelling white farmers. As a result Zimbabwe suffered greatly due to a loss in farming talent. Supposedly some of these farmers settled in Zambia where they're now contributing heavily to the countries agricultural output.

It is for these reasons why we must not be tempted to paint with a broad brush and be careful not to alienate those Europeans who sincerely love and appreciate Africa while respecting the Blackman.

One thing we must always remember is that the end of slavery and the end of colonization did not occur simply because of the efforts of black people. Matter of fact, if it were exclusively a black only effort, we would probably still be fighting those same battles today. There were some abolitionists that weren't black. There were some Europeans who loved Africa and who spoke out (and still are) about the exploitation of the African continent. Just as there are some white men and women in America who fight for the plight of the Blackman. Bernie Sanders being one who easily comes to mind. Decades before he was a presidential candidate, he advocated for civil rights. A very unpopular position to take in the 1960s. He was one of those at the forefront marching with civil rights leaders. White men and women are often unsung heroes of racial equality. We must never be so naïve as to marginalize those who fight for us with us.

In conclusion, Africa never went wrong. Africa never fell from grace. The brilliance that built the great pyramids still exists today. The vast resources still exist today. Our priorities are simply different. Whether or not this is a good thing is debatable. However, I think there is something to be said about the wisdom in the simplicity of the African way. People from all over the world travel to Africa to see animals in the wild, to see huge patches of land that have been untouched, to marvel at the pureness of the way of life. Where food is real food, where the air is clear, where family matters, where the majority of people still talk to each other instead of being buried in electronic devices, where the night sky is filled with stars.

Maybe the Africans are on to something - Maybe a non-material world is the epitome of civilization - Maybe if the western world wouldn't try to 'advance' food, we wouldn't have cancer - Maybe if the western world didn't pursue industrialization we wouldn't have climate change – Maybe the Africans laid back 'non-advancement' approach is right – Maybe Africans would outlive the rest of the world if they weren't attacked by modern mystery diseases such as AIDS and EBOLA – where do these diseases even come from?

Africa was blindsided by the imperial nature of European policy. Africans trusted European intentions and invested in the spiritual world while losing material possessions. To this day, the majority of Africans care more about the afterlife than they do this life. Arguably, rightfully so. Except at some point we must question why those who teach us religion acquire material wealth on earth whilst telling us our riches are in heaven.

I have never seen another group of people more willing to suffer in the name of God. It's almost as though they view economics as spiritual and not practical. Very similar to the older generation of the

African-American tribe who continue to tithe even while suffering. However, I just don't think Gods plan is for anyone to suffer. We should view suffering as evidence of something terribly wrong.

BAD LEADERS

Watch out for those 'leaders' who profit from fueling a divide between the African-American tribe and other local communities. Those who literally 'pimp' the past and current suffering for financial gain. Those leaders with a segregationist world view.

Segregation doesn't work. Separate but equal will never be equal. That debate has already been litigated by a generation of civil rights leaders much smarter than ours.

The practicality of segregation has already been tested in America and in Africa – it doesn't work – black people will always get the short end of the stick. Don't even try it!

True economic emancipation requires leveraging all available economies. Many African countries came to the realization of interdependent economies after colonial independence. They assumed their economies could function seamlessly without outsiders, but that just wasn't the case. Just one example - The African tourism and Arts industries would not exist if it was not for outsiders. These industries support a slew of other businesses such as retail and food businesses.

Any person teaching you to self-segregate from other communities is leading you down a losing path and simply doesn't understand the complexity of local economics.

Supporting community businesses should not mean isolating yourself from the opportunity of generating revenues or seeking employment outside your community. Seeking better employment opportunities outside your community is not selling out. It's common sense. Likewise, fashioning your business to cater to people outside your community is not selling out. It's good business sense. Chinese restaurants don't thrive because of the support of Chinese nationals only, they thrive because they cater to everyone. However, we shouldn't forget to support our own communities in the process.

Unfortunately this has largely been the case. If Gucci, Prada or Louis Vuitton, have not invested in your neighborhood, but Pink Lucy, your neighborhood designer has – that's who should earn your dollars.

The purpose of this book is not to advocate for an African isolationist policy, but to remind the African-American tribe to build a relationship with Africa in addition to other community relationships that already exist.

Be careful not to follow just any leader. Especially in this day and time when everyone is claiming to be 'woke'. Stay away from those who preach hate. Those who are filled with negative energy. Not every white person is racist. Labeling every white person as racist is intellectually dishonest – you don't know every white person. Likewise, not every successful black person is an "uncle tom". Reserve these labels for the people who truly deserve them.

Such leaders will program you to believe in the "struggle". Their intention is to make you live the same painful memory over and over again. Disregarding the reality that human beings need joy to fulfill their purpose. They will make you believe that pain and suffering legitimizes your "blackness", and that any success achieved means you've somewhat "sold out".

Be unapologetic about your success. It's ridiculous for the average young brotha from the suburbs, to feel the need to identify himself as 'hood' just to legitimize his blackness.

Follow leaders with positive energy, those with a positive message that builds you up. Hate and anger are wasted emotions. They serve no other purpose but to destroy the person harboring them. Pride and Joy are the only emotions worth your time.

THE PAIN IS REAL

I
t was July 7th, 2016. A day after I twisted my ankle during a routine workout session. I spent the day mainly just sitting on my couch switching between Netflix and the news. The news was filled with images of protests against police killings of Alton Sterling in Baton Rouge, Louisiana, and Philando Castile in Falcon Heights, Minnesota, which had occurred in the preceding days. Friends of mine and I planned to join the protestors in Dallas that evening, but the pain in my ankle was too much to bare so I decided to sit it out. I was especially bummed because the protest march was just blocks from my apartment building.

I was midway through a movie on Netflix when I heard the sound of a helicopter just outside my window. At first, I didn't think much of it, because I thought it would soon fly by. But the chopping sound went on for more than a minute. At that point, I knew something unusual was happening. I hopped myself to my balcony, trying not to put too much pressure on my ankle. I slid the balcony door open and immediately noticed that it was not just one helicopter, but three. The sight and sound of the helicopters hovering overhead were like something I had only seen in a movie.

My apartment was on the twenty-third floor of a High Rise building downtown Dallas. I looked down over the edge of my balcony to try and catch a glimpse of what had warranted the attention of several choppers. I saw dozens of police vehicles, the most I've ever seen at any one time. Almost every street as far as I could see had a police car. The flashing police lights down the streets looked like a river of Christmas lights. I knew something serious was happening.

I hobbled back to my couch. I switched back to the news and just as I had suspected, Downtown Dallas was the headline. The headlines mentioned gunmen opened fire during the protests. My first thought was that a white supremacist had opened fire on the protestors. I sat there watching in complete shock. I couldn't believe this was happening in my city, let alone just a couple of blocks from me. I called my friends who were attending the protest, and thankfully they were all ok. I turned my attention back to the news and spent the next couple of hours switching from the news to hobbling over to my balcony to see if I could catch a glimpse of what was going on.

The Dallas police Chief, David Brown, held several short press conferences giving periodic updates on the situation. At first, news reports had mentioned several shooters, but later on, they confirmed that it was only one shooter – he shot several police officers, killing five officers and injuring nine others. The shooting was the deadliest incident for U.S. law enforcement since the September 11 attacks.

The shooter was later identified as 25-year-old Xavier Johnson – a black man. Following the shooting, Johnson fled inside a building on the campus of El

Centro College. Police followed him, and a standoff ensued. Johnson said he would speak to black police officers only. He also said that he acted alone and was not part of any group. According to Chief Brown, Johnson appeared delusional, and police saw no possibility of negotiating further. Police killed Johnson with a bomb attached to a remote control bomb disposal robot.

My heart bled for the fallen police officers. They were just there doing their job. I couldn't imagine the pain their family members felt when they learnt that their loved ones were not coming home.

I sat there in disbelief. "Why?" was the question that kept running through my mind. Why did this young brotha choose to physically attack police officers? I suspected that his motivation might have been the recent police killings, but Dallas police wasn't even involved in the police killings. I couldn't comprehend how any Blackman serious to see change would risk demonizing the peaceful protests by caring out such an act. Every black civil leader was outraged by the recent police shootings of unarmed civilians, but we didn't advocate for violence of any kind against police officers. There are other peaceful ways to voice frustration with the system. I just couldn't, and still can't justify his actions. However I understood his pain. I understood how the recent events of police involved killings, could push an already disturbed blackman over the edge.

I logged onto my social media feed and was astonished to see two totally different groups of thought. Some people empathized with the plight of the slain officers, while others empathized with the

35

shooter. I wondered how anyone could empathize with someone who had just committed such an atrocity. I read the opposing comments in disbelief. The people who empathized with the shooter without condemning his actions were absolutely wrong. While I understood their frustration, injuring or taking the life of another is where we should all draw a hard line. Anyone who crosses that line has lost all right to fight or to represent any social justice movement.

However, I couldn't ignore the fact that the pain of hundreds of years of police bullying and a lot more, was real. Even though I disagreed with it, I understood why some people felt no empathy for the slain officers.

This is the mistake America makes - it continues to ignore the real pain that people of color experience daily.

Ever too often, black people in pain are dismissed as "Thugs" and "troublemakers" when they gather as protestors voicing their grievances. Rightwing conservatives often point to successful minorities as evidence of a working system, and that those who aren't successful are responsible for their own suffering or feel "entitled".

But the pain people feel as it relates to the fear or dislikes for the police, is not only about their socio-economic status. Every class of black men, from Harvard professors to twelve-year-old boys have a fear of the police. This is not coincidental. This fear is born of real life encounters. Black women and children are not exempt from this treatment.

Most recently Jacqueline Craig, 46 and her daughter Brea Hymond, 19, of Fort Worth Texas, were arrested and charged with resisting arrest and interfering with public duties. Those charges stemmed from an incident when Fort Worth Police Officer William Martin responded to a report that a male neighbor had assaulted Jacqueline's 7-year-old son. The arrests were captured on cellphone camera which was posted on Facebook live. In the video, Jacqueline tells the officer that her son said he was grabbed and choked by a neighbor. The neighbor said the boy had thrown litter on the ground.

"Why don't you teach your son not to litter?" the officer asks Jaqueline.

"He can't prove to me that my son littered", Jaqueline says. "But it doesn't matter if he did or didn't, it doesn't give him the right to put his hands on him."

"Why not?" the officer responds.

Understandably the situation escalates, as Jaqueline takes offense at the line of questioning and begins raise her voice at the officer at which point the officer says "if you keep yelling at me, you're gonna piss me off, and I'm gonna put you in jail." Brea, Jaqueline's daughter walks in between the officer and her mother as if to move her mother away from the situation. At this point, the officer then moves to arrest Jaqueline. The officer pulls out a stun gun and wrestles Jaqueline and her daughter to the ground and puts them under arrest.

It was difficult for me to watch that video without feeling anger towards that Officer. A 7-year-old was allegedly assaulted by a grown man, and the Officer had the audacity to say "why not?"

His mother did the right thing by not taking matters into her own hands, but rather calling the police for assistance, but instead, she got arrested! The white neighbor who allegedly assaulted her son wasn't even as much as questioned by the officer. In my opinion, there was absolutely nothing that family could've done differently. Some may say "well, she shouldn't have raised her voice at the police officer," but what kind of society do we live in when a black woman raising her voice "pisses off" a police officer more than a white man assaulting a 7-year old ?

This is why some black people don't trust the police. This is why there is a real fear for the police. I understand that the police have a difficult job, and I commend and appreciate those who do their job with great integrity without racism. However, I myself, a middle-class college educated Blackman experience real fear and anxiety when I see a police car behind me. My fear isn't imagined. It's as a result of a combination of watching what's going on in the news and having personally experienced being singled out by the police for absolutely no reason. An experience many black men share.

I remember once traveling to Galveston for the weekend with about eight friends. We were in our twenties at the time, none of us had ever been to a beach. One weekend I came up with the bright idea that we should all go visit the nearest beach. We traveled in two separate cars. The trip to Galveston was fun, but the fun was short lived when we were pulled over by a police officer. Obviously, since both cars in our convoy were traveling together when one car stopped, the other followed suit.

I didn't think much of it, except the police officer is probably just going to ask my friend for his driver's license and proof of insurance and we will be on our way. We sat there waiting for approximately five to ten minutes, wondering what was taking the officer so long to get out of his Vehicle. We then noticed what couldn't have been less than five other police cars pull up. One pulled up about a block ahead of me, the other was on the other side of the street, and the rest were behind us. I have never felt fear like that in my life. Even though I knew I did nothing wrong, I thought that maybe my friends in the car behind me had done something to warrant such a response. A couple police officers walked towards my car, while some stood around my friend's car. There was complete silence in my car. Everyone was terrified. One police officer approached my window and asked for my driver's license and proof of insurance. Another walked around the car peeking inside. The officer then walked back to his vehicle to verify my information. He then went to speak to the other officers who were talking to my friend in the other car. After their short discussion, he walked back to my car and handed me my driver's license and proof of insurance then proceeded to ask me where we were from and where we were headed. I guess maybe trying probe for consistency with what my friend told the other officer. I told him we were traveling from Dallas and none of us had ever seen a beach, so we decided to drive to Galveston. My story must have been consistent with what my friend in the other car said, because the police officer just said, "You're free to go." The officers returned to their vehicles and drove off one at a time. First the police cars that were behind us, then the one across the street, then the one that was a block ahead of us. We then pulled away, no one really saying anything. I picked up my cell phone and called my friend in the car behind me. I asked him if they gave him a ticket. He said no, the officer just asked him for proof of insurance and that was it. I then asked, "why did he pull you over?". He's response was "he didn't say, and I was too terrified to even ask." The experience was painful and traumatizing, because I felt like we were singled out because we were eight young black men traveling together. Minorities understand the fear felt in those moments. I suspect most of my white friends might not see the big deal.

I could tell you about at least four other incidents similar to this, but the point is already made. This is just how it is to be a black man in America. Almost every Blackman I know has a similar story. Some a lot worse.

So even though I don't agree with hate for police officers, I understand why there is fear and mistrust. It's not imagined. It's not something that happens only to criminals. Even law abiding good citizens get "the treatment." So when we see a Blackman being gunned down or choked to death by police officers, we sincerely feel hurt, because we all understand that unless something changes, that could easily be anyone of us.

If the black middle class who have experienced success and are living relatively comfortable lives fear the police, just imagine how a black person living in poverty feels?

In this society filled with so many images of black

success, it's easy to forget that there are millions of black families who live in poverty. Imagine the psyche of a family of which every generation since slavery, has never been above poverty – in the richest country on earth. By today's definition, this would mean a family of four (mother, father, and two kids) with an annual income of $23,550. I personally know many families who fit into that category. I'm sure you do too.

Picture a black person dealing with the daily challenges of police harassment, racism, crime and violence, seeing images of black people being killed at the hands of police, going through life knowing that every generation of their family has never experienced the so called "American dream". Eventually one would reach a boiling point.

Frankly, I think the level of humility expressed by the African-American tribe is admirable given the circumstances. Protestors are crying out for the ruling class to take notice of their plight. The pain is real. Even successful black people feel the pain because they realize that their success is not the norm – they got lucky or blessed, depending on your interpretation – because we all know hard work isn't the only ingredient to success.

BLACK-ON-BLACK 'PHENOMENA'

O ne can't truly speak about the relationship between the African-American tribe and police without speaking about black-on-black crime. The rationale often heard from the Right criticizing groups like Black Lives Matter is centered on the argument that black-on-black crime takes more lives than police involved shootings and yet the African-American tribe doesn't appear to be as outraged.

At first glance, it may appear as though those who make this argument have somewhat of a point, but a deeper, simple analysis of the facts proves otherwise. Ponder this – what do you find more outrageous, a criminal committing a murder or a police officer committing a murder? If you're like any other reasoning human being, you'll probably say that murder, in general, is outrageous, but it's especially horrendous when the people sworn to protect the community act like criminals themselves. This is precisely why people gather in protest when even just one person is killed by a police officer. The protests are in response to a system that seemingly doesn't have justice for black victims, but instead responds by demonizing the victims.

Furthermore, the entire 'phenomenon' of black-on-black crime is not a phenomenon at all. Society evidently promotes negative community narratives as "black problems" when in reality they aren't unique to black communities at all.

Murder is typically perpetrated by someone close to a victim. This 'closeness' could be family relations, business relations, community associations, etc. This is true in every community and not just in a black American community. As we have black-on-black crime, there also exists white-on-white crime, Asian-on-Asian crime, African-on-African crime, Husband-on-wife crime, etc.

I'm not trying to take away from the severity of the problem, but simply pointing out the hypocrisy in the narrative.

If anyone is truly interested in solving the so-called 'black-on-black' crime problem, then one needs to solve the source of the problem – lack of opportunity.

I've been fortunate enough to have risen out of poverty. I'm the first in my family to graduate from college. Every day I thank God for my good fortune because I know it wasn't a result of just hard work. There was plenty luck, help from others and supernatural intervention involved.

I spent many years pondering how I could give back to a country that had given me so much. I pondered what I could do to honor the people who came before me. Slave ancestors, abolitionists, civil rights leaders, etc. All those who made it possible for me to have the freedoms I have today, that I may even write this as a first generation African-American. I pondered how I too could make a difference for the next generation. Always thinking of what the next 100 years will be like for people who look like me. Conscious of the fact that there's equally someone else probably planning a future that disregards people like me. Someone else is planning a future where Africans and African-Americans remain separate, where Africa remains in poverty, and where no matter what African-Americans achieve, they will still remain second class citizens. I know this because the oppressive policies we experience didn't happen by accident, someone authored them.

My close friend Shanika and I would speak of visions of the future of how we would start an international organization, build a school, rub elbows with people we admired like of Oprah and the Obama's, all in an effort to give back and help others strategize for the future. Clearly, dreams beyond our resources. But that didn't stop us from dreaming and doing. Our ambition was never about making money or becoming rich, it was always about (and still is) about helping others. Our passion for our mission was so strong that we didn't even consider asking others for financial support. We kick started the Community Scholars initiative using our own resources.

Our primary goal was to help an entire generation break through the psychological bondage that came with poverty. We were going to solve the opportunity problem by sharing that which helped us overcome it - reading.

We sourced the root of all psychological bondage

experienced by people of color to a lack of knowledge and belief in self, caused by centuries of racial oppression. The racial oppression that continues today but has evolved into covert, subtle, systemic policies, masked as good intentions.

Many believe the key to success is education, and the lack of "education" is the number one reason people are in poverty. This is true, however, (and unfortunately) what having an "education" has come to mean in today's society is having paid absorbent amounts of money to learn something you probably can learn for free through self-study.

Our epiphany was an obvious one – help people learn for free.

It never made sense to me, and it probably won't make sense to you too, if you really think about, why is it that we pay these extremely high tuition costs to just sit in a classroom and listen to someone speak? I can understand some cost to maintain the infrastructure, and maybe salaries for the professors, but even with that, in this day and time when we have online courses, why are we still paying these absorbent rates? One could probably learn more from watching YouTube videos and independent study than sitting in a classroom. After all, that's precisely what professors try to teach us – research and study.

I understand I'm overly simplifying the college experience, and high tuition costs cover important STEM programs, but just looking back at my liberal arts degree, I honestly can't think of one class that I couldn't have passed without ever stepping foot in a classroom. All I needed to do was read. So what are we paying for?

Our mission was simple, we were going to promote reading and study in a way that made sense. We were going to read with purpose. We were going to give intellectual confidence back to the people six pages a day.

I reached out to my other friend Nicole, who was passionate about community activism and together we formed "6 pages a day – The Urban Reading Club." The concept was simply to build a community of avid readers by simply reading 6 pages a day.

The beginning was rough because we were approaching community activism from an angle that people just weren't familiar with. To many, it just seemed like we weren't doing enough. "Reading" just seemed so boring and weak. The group wasn't charismatic, it wasn't as vocal as other groups, but we had faith in our approach because we knew that we were building intellectual confidence – the foundation of any successful society.

Rather than allowing a whole generation of community leaders to intellectually disregard themselves because they didn't have an opportunity for a formal college education, we revealed the truth about what it means to be an intellectual. Our goal is to spread this message to the masses. Targeting especially those who can't afford a formal college education. Naturally, the group attracted like-minded individuals of all educational backgrounds. Soon we had cross-pollination of those with a formal education and those without. Our long term goal is to meet the requirements for accreditation, so that we may one day be able to formally recognize the intellectual advancements of our members by providing actual degrees.

"GREATEST"
ACCORDING
TO WHO?

I was born in Springfield Missouri to African parents. When I was only months old, my family decided to move back to Africa. I grew up there. I did all my primary and secondary education in Africa – Zambia to be exact.

My father used to tell me how lucky I was to be an 'American.' I was the only one in my family to be born in America, so I was 'The American.' I was proud to be American, and still am. I grew up watching TV shows that I later found out were the same TV shows that were popular in America. I watched the Cosby's, Different Strokes, Good Times, The Jefferson's, Fresh Prince of Bel Air, etc. So did every other kid in Zambia who had a TV.

Almost all the music I listened to, was American. My childhood heroes were Michael Jackson, MC Hammer, Bobby Brown, Snoop Dog, Dr. Dre, etc. I tried to mimic the dance moves, I rapped, I would change my accent and try to talk like them.

Now keep in mind all this was happening while I was in Africa. The very same Africa, you probably envy and revere for being the epitome of culture – and it is. I was surrounded by an abundance of culture and age-old traditions. Yet when I turned on the TV, right there before me was this other culture; an undeniably dominant and powerful culture.

Just think about it - here are these men and women, descendant from slavery, who had their culture, names, traditions ripped away, but were now influencing and inspiring African children with this 'New culture' - I would argue the most influential culture the world has ever seen. A culture more influential than that of the English. A "black" culture taking over the world without the use of guns or war. People from all corners of the earth, fully aware of their own ancient cultures, still gravitate to this new culture. A culture, whose influence has even surpassed the cultures of those who enslaved it's architects. A culture that is now the "American" brand around the world.

The phenomenon of the African-American tribe is an amazing phenomenon when you really think of it. Very rarely in human history does a culture spread without the use of force or violence. Frankly, the only other time I can think of that happening at a similar scale was probably the Asians with their martial arts. To be fair, European culture has spread too, but to be fairer, there was a lot of arm twisting to say it lightly.

So what is African-American culture? And why is it that so many in the tribe don't bask in the glory of arguably the greatest culture the world has ever seen? Why do so many in the tribe feel as though they don't have a culture? So many have flocked to religion or new age 'conscious' groups to try and identify with something. Meanwhile, people in Africa, Europe, the

Middle East, etc. are all trying to be 'cool' like the African-American tribe.

Personally, I think there are two reasons why people in the tribe may not feel the pride as rightfully theirs. First, being that historically there's been a conscious effort within America to mute African-American cultural pride.

We see it all the time. For example, if an African-American has a name that is unique to African-American culture, then that person may be marginalized when seeking employment. Often you'll hear people say, "Don't give your child that ghetto name unless you don't want them ever to get a job."

Another example is language. African-Americans will often come up with new terms to mean different things, but rather than embrace the evolution in language; their new terms are discredited as slangs. However on the flipside, when Eurocentric elitists come up with a new term it is made official and added to the dictionary.

What's even more shocking is that the African-American tribe would create some new cultural phenomenon, as they often do, and the Eurocentric elite class would shun the phenomenon as being in poor taste or some other ridiculous elitist bullshit, but later on adopt that same phenomenon as theirs. We've seen this happen with rock, jazz, rap and more recently we've seen it happen with the dance style of twerking.

The same pattern in the fashion industry exists. Cultural fashion trends that are born of the African-American tribe are often marginalized until some corporation takes notice and exploits it for financial gain.

So it's hard to feel proud of your culture when every time you are told that your culture is inferior – "Hood," "Rachett," "Ghetto," are some of the terms used to discredit the genius and originality of the African-American tribe.

I speak not only as an African-American tribe member born here but also as someone who grew up in Africa. Spending more than 17 years on each continent, I see things from both inside and outside the box. Which leads me to the second reason why some African-Americans may not feel cultural pride – Exposure.

I always say, 'If you're an African-American and you want to see just how great your culture is, then you need to travel outside the U.S. You need to go out of the country and experience how other people treat you. You need to experience the admiration for the way you talk, your fashion sense, your music choice and just everything about you. People around the world LOVE black America. Even the negative side of it. I remember traveling in Africa and seeing all these kids and grown folks too, who have never seen gang banging (granted this isn't exclusive to black culture), calling themselves gangstas and thugs because of the influence of gansta rap. It's like African-American culture can't do any wrong. However with this great gift of influence comes great responsibility – something I'll address in a later book.

It's a refreshing thing to see because being in America sometimes, one feels like being black is a curse. Simple tasks like taking a walk in the neighborhood make me nervous because I don't want to make other people nervous; simply because I'm

Black. I often have to be cautious about taking a walk after dark in my neighborhood for fear of looking suspicious. Mind you, this is a neighborhood I've lived in for seven years, but I know that I'll always look suspicious.

The only time I get pleasant "Hellos" is when I'm not wearing unique black cultural attire – hip hop attire - you know –Jordans', a Hoodie, etc. However when I'm in classic European wear – "dressed like a white boy" my friends would say, people in my neighborhood would appear a little more at ease around me.

Ironically when I wear my African garb, everyone loves it – I'm no longer just a "Blackman" I am "African," and somehow, that's less threatening. I find it interesting that people embrace African culture but find African-American culture threatening. Maybe it's the guilt associated with slavery, who knows.

EXTRAORDINARY CULTURE

I t wouldn't be right for me to keep speaking about "the most influential culture" without offering some historic evidence of the extraordinary achievements of the culture.

One cannot speak about the African-American tribe without speaking of the Harlem Renaissance. The Harlem Renaissance was the name given to the cultural, social, and artistic explosion that took place in Harlem between the end of World War I and the middle of the 1930s. During this period, Harlem was a cultural center, drawing black writers, artists, musicians, photographers, poets, and scholars. Its essence was summed up by critic and teacher Alain Locke in 1926 when he declared through art, "Negro life is seizing its first chances for group expression and self- determination."

(Source: http://www.history.com/topics/black-history/harlem-renaissance)

The nucleus of the movement included Jean Toomer, Langston Hughes, Rudolf Fisher, Wallace Thurman, Jessie Redmon Fauset, Nella Larsen, Arna Bontemps, Countee Cullen, and Zora Neale Hurston. An older generation of writers and intellectuals–James Weldon Johnson, Claude McKay, Alain Locke, and

Charles S. Johnson–served as mentors. You're probably familiar with the Harlem Renaissance, but for the reader who is not, take a moment to look up each name, view their work, and as you read, remember that what you're reading is the work of people robbed of their culture. These are some of the pioneers who created a brand new commercial culture which we all now share in.

But even before the Harlem Renaissance, was Jazz. Jazz originated in the late 19th to early 20th century, as interpretations of American and European classical music entwined with African and slave folk songs and the influences of West African culture. As jazz spread around the world, it drew on different national, regional, and local musical cultures, which gave rise to many distinctive styles. One of the most influential Jazz artists was an African-American by the name of Louis Armstrong, a trumpeter, composer, singer and occasional actor. His career spanned five decades, from the 1920s to the 1960s, and different eras in jazz. Armstrong was a foundational influence on jazz, shifting the focus of the music from collective improvisation to solo performance. After Jazz came, all sorts of other artistic, musical expressions ranging from Rock and Roll to the Blues and everything in between. Again all created by people robbed of their culture and every aspect of their identity.

Fast forward to the 1970's and another cultural movement known as hip-hop emerged in the predominantly African-American South Bronx section of New York City; with music being the central component of the complex hip-hop culture, which also includes graffiti painting, dance, fashion, etc. The most notable artists at the time included DJ Kool Herc, Grandmaster Flash and The Furious Five, Fab Five Freddy Marley Marl Afrika Bambaataa, Kool Moe Dee, Kurtis Blow, Doug E. Fresh, Whodini, Warp 9, The Fat Boys, and Spoonie Gee. The Sugarhill Gang's 1979 song "Rapper's Delight" is widely regarded to be the first hip-hop record to gain widespread popularity in the mainstream.

The 1980s marked the diversification of hip hop, as the genre developed more complex styles. Before the 1980s, hip-hop music was confined to the United States. However, during the 1980s, it began to spread to music scenes in dozens of countries in Africa, Europe, Asia, Australia, South America, virtually the entire globe was engulfed by hip-hop, many of which mixed it with local styles.

I could go on and on giving you different examples of the impact of the African-American tribe, but it's so evident that one need not look too far to see the truth.

However, we still find many in the African-American tribe who feel as though their culture is nonexistent. "African culture" that is. This longing for an African connection can be both positive and negative. The negative arises when the individual takes no pride in the culture that has developed during the 400-500 years of slavery and post-slavery.

Understandably many who do not feel pride in the achievements of the last four to five hundred years take pride in historic Africa instead. Some of these individuals find themselves leaning into the 'Conscious Community.' A community I identify myself with to some degree. However, I have a three pillar approach to my identity. My three pillars are - **I recognize the majesty of Ancient African cultures, I recognize the realities of present African cultures, and I recognize the brilliance of African-American culture.**

The conscious community are the people who you've probably seen on social networks usually speaking of ancient Egypt or Kemet, Kush, Toubou, etc. They long for a connection with Africa. They speak of Kingdoms and civilizations long lost. Which I think is a beautiful thing. However, I think in the process, they miss the greatness of the present moment. They miss the fact that Africa is present today. It's only a 12 – 16hr flight away. You don't have to go back thousands years to find Africa. They also miss the present moment, the greatest tribe of Africa – the African-American tribe. One doesn't need to go back thousands of years to find greatness in Blackness. It's constantly all around us.

I believe right now, in this present moment, we're experiencing the ripening of the greatest Africans the world has ever seen. **But we must not make the mistake of rating ourselves in comparison to other ethnic groups. We must measure our greatness by what we've overcome.** It is for this reason and by this measure that the African-American tribe is undeniably the greatest tribe of Africa.

The "Greatest" is not a title to disrespect any other African tribe, but rather an acknowledgment of the spirit of the African-American tribe that has fought a good fight.

While it is true that every country and every tribe in Africa has faced enormous challenges brought about mainly by the colonization and civil war, it is also true that no one had to endure anything quite like the people who were taken away from the continent. There's something very different about suffering in your land, among the spirits of your ancestors and being forcibly taken from your land, across a vast ocean, and being sold into slavery, then having to endure centuries of slavery, segregation and now mass incarceration. Constantly fighting against a system that is systemically engineered for your destruction. I don't think anything equals that.

Yet, the tribe of Africans in America has somehow found a way to live through all of that and still develop one of the world's most influential cultures. Arguably more globally influential than any tribe still on the African continent.

However, the lack of a connection to Africa leaves many without the spiritual platform necessary to realize their greatness. Time and time again, I've witnessed a spiritual awakening of sorts when a black person in America embraces Africa and realizes that they're not just a "Nigga" but a descendant of Africa – the envy and aspirational prize of Europeans and Asians.

The African-American story did not begin with slavery and will not end with us. We have a purpose and responsibility to remind ourselves of this. We must look back past slavery, and at the same time look forward past our present time to fully appreciate ourselves. If you're a black person in America, or matter of fact, anywhere else in the world, and you don't have any connection to Africa either in mind or in deed, then your existence will probably be an empty one. Crime, poverty, and disparity can be tied to the lack of education. I'll go one step further and say they're tied to the lack of spiritual connection. For black people this means a lack of an African connection. Mental emancipation comes from loving oneself. One cannot love oneself without knowing yourself. A big part of who we are as black people is Africa. We must embrace Africa.

Africa needs the African-American tribe, and the African-American tribe needs Africa. There's no escaping it.

No matter how much the African-American tribe achieves in the US, they will never be truly free, until they undo what slavery did to our ancestors – we need to establish a connection with Africa.

As it is today, many in the African-American tribe still feel like second class citizens mainly because of systemic racism - a justice system that's sending thousands of black men to prison for nonviolent drug-related offenses at rates that vastly outpace their white counterparts. And also because of an employment system that only works for blacks who 'sanitize' their cultural norms – often having to talk, dress, and act 'proper' which too many times is code for 'white.'

No person can ever experience freedom without economic freedom. And while many in the African-American tribe look to the U.S government for relief, respect, and essentially to 'save' them from the very systems set in place by the bureaucracies in Washington, they should instead start taking a closer look at their own community resources and how they can leverage Africa.

Africa is a treasure chest of investment opportunity. It

is the platform that many in the African-American tribe should consider standing on. Both spiritually and economically.

Unfortunately too many may feel far disconnected from Africa. After all, their parents, grandparents and even great-grandparents may have had no connection to the continent. However, one just needs to visit Africa and walk amongst the people to realize that they are your people. If you were to travel to Africa today, no African would even notice the difference between you and all the other Africans except for your accent. You can literally walk around unnoticed. This applies to light-skinned African-Americans too. Contrary to stereotypes, there is such a thing as light skinned Africans. I happen to be one of them. Your presence in Africa will be no different than a white person from the U.S walking around in any part of Europe - they don't stick out – they're home.

I recently visited Zambia, and I was amazed by the diversity of foreign investment. As soon as I arrived at the airport in the capital city Lusaka, I was greeted by billboards that were both in English and Chinese!

That's right; the Chinese are investing in Africa. Can you imagine that the British, French, Portuguese, Spanish, Indians and now even the Chinese are all in Africa, investing and building wealth, while most in the African-American tribe never have as much as visited Africa? Not even for a vacation?

In my opinion, Africa is still poor because unfortunately, Africans are being bamboozled. Most foreign investors only have their country of origin interests at heart. They come to Africa, they invest in

Africa, they generate great returns on their investments, and then they leave. All those profits leave Africa and go to Britain, China, India, etc. Very little remains to build the continent.

If the African-American tribe invested in Africa together with the Chinese, Indians, British, etc. Africa would be better off because, the African-American tribe, unlike any other foreign nation, might have a vested interest in Africa that goes beyond personal wealth. The legacy of the continent may mean something. The social respect of black people all across the world is tied directly to the success of Africa.

Wealth would flow between communities in the U.S and Africa. There would be a highway of exchange of goods and services, commerce and ideas. African-Americans based in the U.S would immediately notice an emergence of a new economy. A new hustle – doing business with Africa.

Likewise, Africans would establish partnerships with a community that shares a similar vision – the economic emancipation of all black people. This economic highway will bleed over into the Caribbean, then Europe and eventually all over the world, uniting all descendants of Africa; meaning more opportunities and economic prosperity for all people currently living on the continent.

But this will never happen if the African-American tribe – the greatest African tribe, does not take an active leadership role in the advancement of Africa. As long as there's a divide between the African-American tribe and Africans, there will never be one Africa. Europeans know this. You'd have to be living under a rock not to notice the overt effort to keep Africans divided. Divide and conquer is not just a theory but an actual practice employed. It's a strategy that's been used since the beginning of time and continues to be used today.

Stop and think about your childhood, what do you remember you knew about Africa? Or even now, what do you know about Africa? Do you feel pride when you think about Africa, or do you still think "African booty scratcher?" Remember that? "African booty scratcher" was something you never wanted to be. All you probably saw on TV were Africans dying of hunger or running around with no clothes on, etc. Keep in mind that EVERYTHING shown on TV is someone's idea. These are the images they wanted you to see when you saw Africa. This is what they wanted you to absorb. Now stop and think of the images you saw of Greece, Italy, France, etc. That programming is probably still deeply engraved in you. Be honest with yourself, would you rather go on vacation to Paris, France or Cape Town South Africa? If you're like the average African-American, you're probably thinking Paris – and that's ok, if that's your preference, except if it's your preference simply because you don't know enough about Cape Town or you have a fear of Africa. Then you may need to reprogram yourself cognitively; because you're programmed divided from Africa.

In a perfect world, the African-American tribe should be doing business with Africa, vacationing in Africa, investing in Africa, building schools, hospitals, businesses, etc. Most importantly, getting involved in African politics – Again, sharing with Africans what can only be learned after spending 400 years in

America.

Likewise, Africans should welcome African-Americans and teach them the ways of old, reacquaint them with the languages of the trees and the wind, openly share with them cultures and traditions and allow them to participate in African politics - Maybe Africa cannot unite as one due to tribalism and regional bias - Maybe if there is ever to emerge a leader of ALL OF AFRICA, this individual would need to be of-Africa, but not tied to any particular region – Maybe this leader will come from the diaspora. We never know what positive possibilities may result.

While the past is important, we must think about the future. What do the next 200 years look like for black people? The one issue I take with the conscious community is that much of the rhetoric and discussion is focused on the past. I understand that there is a need to connect with one's past but why can't we do both? Why can't we learn from the past and at the same time plan for the future? Remembering who we are is the first step in planning who we're going to be. Somehow the conversation never seems to go past the first step. You're 'woke', now what?

The African-American tribe is the only ethnic group, who do not have an active relationship with their motherland. Take a moment and look around you. All ethnic groups, Jews, Filipinos, Mexicans, Indians, Chinese, etc., all have connections with where they originally came from. And I'm not talking about just a historic connection, I'm talking about an active economic and cultural connection.

Take, for example, Jewish Americans. Some of

these families have been in the U.S for hundreds of years, but they still maintain a real connection to Israel - nation that was formed in the 1940's. Matter of fact they take this connection so seriously that they have non-profit educational organizations that sponsor free ten-day heritage trips to Israel for young adults of Jewish heritage, aged 18–26. Why haven't Africans and the African-American tribe partnered together to do the same? Can you imagine what that would do for the black community? If you've never been to Africa, wouldn't it be nice to be able to go for free, on a ten day well organized educational trip? These are the kinds of ideas we need to be thinking about. Another example is the Filipino people. Did you know that the money sent to the Philippines by the over 10 million Filipino expatriate workers accounts for about 10% of the countries entire economy? With these types of investments in self, where do you think the Jews and the Filipinos will be in the next 100 years? Now, what are we doing as African-Americans?

I remember reading a book by Ta-Nehisi Coates, a great writer, titled "Between the World and Me." The book is basically a letter to his son. In it, he describes the different hurdles African-Americans have to go through. He uses his own experiences as well as experiences of others. It's a really good book, except at the end I couldn't help but feel "Wow, being black sucks." And this is the problem we have today in the Black world. We have so much going on that we forget to remind ourselves that being black is a blessing and not a curse. However, our focus has been so much on how 'they' treat us, what 'they' do or do not do to help us, how 'they' stole from us, etc. We're constantly victims - in Africa and America. And while that's very true, we need to change the way we think of ourselves. The victim narrative is depressing and draining. I remember finishing the book and just feeling defeated like there was no hope for the black man anywhere in the world. I almost felt ashamed for walking around in this 'black body.' But that needs to stop.

OPPORTUNITIES
IN AFRICA

We're not our past or current circumstance. We carry forward the victories and lessons from the past. Not the despair or shame. We are what we say we are. The system wants you to think you're a victim. It wants you to feel helpless. It wants you to feel small and ill-equipped to compete.

As cliché as it sounds, this reminds me of the story of David and Goliath. Goliath was a giant trained to kill with lots of military experience. Even the most experienced fighters in Saul's Army were afraid to come up against Goliath. Then here comes David, a sheep herder volunteering to take on Goliath. When David was asked if he had any military experience, he said, "No…but your servant has killed both the lion and the bear…" See, David didn't see himself as a victim, but as a conqueror, and because he knew that God was on his side, he knew he could stand up against Goliath. In the same way, even though the black world has not defeated our Goliath – economic freedom; we have already defeated slavery, segregation, colonialization and apartheid. So now what's left for black people to be truly equal to the rest of the world, is for us to have economic freedom. This starts by supporting black businesses in the US and Africa. For example, an African-American should be able to go to a African-American jeweler to purchase an engagement ring, and that jeweler should have a connection in Africa who supplies the diamonds. Again, there should be a direct economic highway between Africa and the African-American tribe. This is how the communal economies of Jews, Chinese, and Indians work. They primarily support businesses in their community. And their community does not mean just their neighborhood; it's global.

For too long African-Americans have felt as though they're not part of this African family, but I can't stress enough that, that is a lie. Peter Tosh, the Reggae singer, said it best in his song "African," he said

"Don't care where you come from
As long as you're a black man, you're an African
No mind your nationality
You have got the identity of an African."

African-Americans need to embrace the reality of a global economy. For example, If you're a small business owner in the U.S, and you're in the business of selling second-hand affordable shoes, you may not have much of a market in your local community, but if you had a connection in Africa to market them for you, you would be in business without physicaly having to be in Africa.

There's an unlimited number of businesses that can't exist solely in the US economy, but that are possible when partnering with Africa. Ever wonder why so many Africans who come to the U.S are so successful? It's mainly because they take advantage of the global economy. I know an African brotha who collects old toasters, microwaves, mixers, etc., just any old kitchen appliance that people in the U.S give away for free while updating their kitchen. He ships them to Africa where his brother has a kitchen appliance store.

Think about it; He collects the appliances for free. His only expense is the shipping cost, which isn't too bad because of he ships in bulk, and then sells in Africa for what's pretty much all profit. That's an opportunity that arose as a result of a global economy.

Just the other day, I had a friend in Africa ask me if I was interested in purchasing gold in small quantities. He's literally digging up Gold using a pick and a shovel. An opportunity I'm definitely interested in pursuing once I do my homework. So again, my point being, there is no downside to embracing Africa. We simply can't even quantify how many opportunities would arise for the African-America tribe once everyone starts taking Africa seriously, all we know is that there will be many opportunities.

The biggest mistake any African-American can do is believe he/she is simply "American." We've seen several black celebrities over the years reject the notion that they're African and only embrace their American side because that's all they've known. But again, stop and observe that while these black people reject Africa, Italian Americans, Jewish Americans, Indian Americas are all embracing their roots, and as a result, they're a stronger knit community. Additionally, while some African-Americans are rejecting Africa, the Chinese, British, etc. are in Africa building wealth.

So again I ask, what do you think the next 100 years

will look like for black people? If history has taught us anything, it's that no one is looking out for us, but us. So don't look to any other ethnic group to solve the problems that we currently have. In some cases, they created and continued to perpetuate the problems.

If things keep going the way they are for the next 100 years, the African-American tribe will still be fighting for equal opportunities in the US, while the Chinese will have taken over Africa. Right now as I write this China is investing in bridges, roads, airports in Africa. They have a long term plan.

As I mentioned earlier, even though I was born in the U.S, I literally grew up in Africa. I did first to twelfth grade there. My perspective on Africa is not one of someone who just visited for a couple of weeks, only saw the good or the bad, and decided to write a book – No. I lived there, I learned there, I speak a couple of languages, I know the people, and I know the traditions. I've observed the strengths and weaknesses.The same is true with the US. I was born here, I've lived here just as long as I've lived in Africa. I've lived in the hood, I've lived in luxury apartments, I've experienced the American struggle, I've experienced American success, I know discrimination, I went to college here. I've observed the strengths and weaknesses.

My educational background is in political science so I have a decent understanding of how to evaluate political and social systems.My point being that I know firsthand, the pros and cons of both continents. The choice is not between here or there - your mindset needs to be **here AND there**.

THE MESSENGER

I grew up in Zambia, a country in southern Africa. Most people have never heard of Zambia. Probably because Zambia is one of those African countries that never makes the news in a good or bad way. Zambia is a peaceful nation. Despite the struggle for independence from British colonial rule, Zambians have never fought a war. Zambia is the African country that has so much love and peace that it simply doesn't appeal to the mainstream media. The western media seems to only have an appetite for drama, chaos, famine, etc. when covering Africa.

Think about it. If I were to ask you to list the African countries, your list would probably start with Ethiopia, Somalia, and Nigeria. Countries which have made some negative headline. Your list may contain other countries as well, but that's probably because you know someone from those countries or you're simply a well-informed person. But my point is that the average American cannot look at a map of Africa and name every single country. Something I think every black person should be able to do.

Zambia is a beautiful country. I always tell people that it has some kind of magic to it. It's hard to describe, but if you ever visit, as soon as your plane touches down and you walk outside and breathe that Zambian air for the first time, you'll know exactly what I mean. It might just be that the air is so fresh and there's barely any pollution that you just get a high off of fresh air; who knows.

I grew up in Livingstone, a small town in the southern province of Zambia. This is my ancestral homeland. My mother's side of the family is part of the Mukuni royal family. Mukuni is a small village set out in one of the most beautiful landscapes. I honestly didn't fully appreciate the beauty of Livingstone or my heritage until I came to the U.S.

Growing up I took for granted the fact that the 7th natural wonder of the world, 'Victoria Falls,' was right in my backyard. Most people I've met in the US, have never even heard of Victoria Falls. As far as they're concerned, Niagara Falls is the world's largest waterfall. It isn't. The mighty Victoria Falls is.

I took for granted its beauty and grandiosity, especially during the rainy season when the river waters are full. The sound of falling water is like nothing you've ever heard. The local name for Victoria Falls is "Mosi-oa-tunya," literally meaning "the smoke that thunders."

The mist that forms as billions of gallons of water hit the rocks below, is like nothing you've ever seen. There's an everlasting rainbow formed above the waterfall. It looks like something of fairytales.

In early November 1855, David Livingstone, the first European to see the waterfall traveled down the Zambezi River to see for himself the area the natives called "smoke that thunders." Approaching the spot in canoes, the party could see the columns of spray and hear the thunderous roar of water miles away from the falls. He described what he saw in his journal as a "sight so lovely angels must have gazed upon in their flight."

"After twenty minutes' sail from Kalai, we came in sight, for the first time, of the columns of vapor appropriately called 'smoke,' rising at a distance of five or six miles, exactly as when large tracts of grass are burned in Africa. Five columns now arose, and, bending in the direction of the wind, they seemed placed against a low ridge covered with trees; the tops of the columns at this distance appeared to mingle with the clouds. They were white below, and higher up became dark, so as to simulate smoke very closely. The whole scene was extremely beautiful; the banks and islands dotted over the river are adorned with sylvan vegetation of great variety of color and form...no one can imagine the beauty of the view from anything witnessed in England. It had never been seen before by European eyes; but scenes so lovely must have been gazed upon by angels in their flight. The only want felt is that of mountains in the background. The falls are bounded on three sides by ridges 300 or 400 feet in height, which are covered with forest, with the red soil appearing among the trees."
(Source http://www.eyewitnesstohistory.com/livingstone.htm)

I took for granted what made Africa "Africa" – the untouched beauty. Animals in the wild and human beings existing together. I remember every other weekend, my friends and I would ride our bikes to the Victoria Falls. That was our chill spot. We would walk down to the bottom of the waterfall to a spot called the "boiling pot." I assume it got its name from the way the water would rush down and smack on the rocks with such velocity over and over again in different directions that it would create a bounce and a swirl similar to water boiling in a pot. The best part was the walk down the gorge to the spot. The mist from the waterfall had created a little rain forest in the middle of nowhere. The vegetation was thick, luscious and always green. Just as you would imagine when you think of a jungle.

The path to the bottom was an experience in itself. I remember running into baboons several times. Now if you've never seen a baboon you need to google a picture. A baboon is a monkey with a face of a dog – at least how I see them. These baboons were everywhere! There must've been hundreds of them. They wouldn't bother you if you didn't bother them. Just don't have any kind of food, or loose items on you, because these suckers were like stealing human beings. They're highly intelligent. Remember the Disney cartoon Aladdin? Remember how smart his monkey was? No kidding, baboons are like that in real life.

One day as my friends and me were walking down to the boiling pot along the narrow path, we ran into a herd of baboons. The Alpha male calmly came down from a tree and just sat in the middle of the path. Looking at us as though saying "I dare you to try and pass." Keep in mind I was probably only twelve years old at the time, and the oldest person in our crew couldn't have been older than fourteen. So there we were five kids, in the middle of this 'jungle' facing off with hundreds of baboons and especially this big Alpha baboon that was directly in front of us. One of my friends tried to reach for a rock. I distinctively remember another friend saying "Usa Yese" basically meaning "don't even try."

See the thing about baboons and monkeys, in

general, is that they're known to mimic your actions. So if you start throwing rocks, you risk a hundred baboons throwing rocks right back at you. So we just stood there in a stare off that lasted probably a minute but felt like hours. I guess he made his point and just decided to move on. That was a huge relief.

You'd think we would just turn around and go home after an encounter such as that. But no, things like that were normal. Encounters with animals in the wild are just part of everyday life in Africa. We continued down to the boiling pot and enjoyed the day doing nothing but just enjoying the scenery. Google "boiling pot Zambia" and you'll see what I mean.

(I thought of including a picture of what I'm asking you to google, but I decided against it, as my intention is that I motivate you to explore Africa beyond this book.)

On our way back to the main town, I remember encountering a herd of elephants. We were riding our bicycles along the main road, and they were crossing the road. Something very common in Livingstone.

The smart thing for us to do would've been just to stop and wait till they cross. The dumb thing was to try and weave through the herd - which was exactly what we did. Scariest moment of my life.

We left the boiling pot around 7 pm. The sun was still shining, but it had started to go down. We hopped on our bicycles and started to ride down the main road heading home. The main road was tarred. It was narrow by American standards, it barely had enough room for cross traffic. We rode in a single line, with the fastest rider in the front and of course the slowest rider at the back - which just happened to be me. I was the fat kid growing up.

As we rode, my mind wandered like it always did. I remember just taking it all in as though knowing one day I will miss it. Both sides of the road were bush. Dry grass, some small trees, and a couple of baobab trees.

Most people I've met in the US have never heard of a baobab tree. It's magical. Something else that looks like it's out of a fairy tale. I always say if magic ever existed it would be found around baobab trees. Google them, you'll see what I mean.

As we rode, I noticed the pace picking up rather aggressively. I didn't think too much about it, because the fellas would typically race to see who would make it home faster. I being the slowest person in the group, just wanted not to be left too far behind. When they rode faster, I rode faster.

There I was peddling as fast as I could, trying to keep up with the person ahead of me. Then I saw a trunk and a huge head peered out of the bushes to my right. It was an elephant. Before I could process the severity of the situation or say anything, I saw another, and another. They were on the road, calming crossing. I thought I was going to die. I looked ahead, and I could see my friends pretty much weaving past one and another, and I was following suit. It was too late to stop now.

All that went through my mind was that we needed to get the heck out of there as fast as possible. The entire episode probably lasted 10 seconds, but we continued to ride as fast as we could, all the way home. No one stopped to look back.

The entire time my mind kept on telling me "it's right behind you." But truth be told, those elephants were calm as can be, minding their own business and probably didn't even notice us. We all arrived at my home at the exact same time. I remember the guys bust out into laughter once they saw that we all made it. They laughed especially at me because I was the fat, slow kid. One of the guys joked saying "I just knew those elephants had you." Another one said, "I didn't know you could ride that fast." We laughed about it, and the next weekend we did it again.

When I think about Africa, these are the memories that come to mind. It's beautiful, it's real, and it's simple. Every day is a vacation. Every day is an adventure. "Life" is abundant. One has to travel to the western world to experience modern slavery to really appreciate Africa. Africans themselves don't know how good they have it. I often tell my family in Africa that the only goal they have is putting food on the table – that's a beautiful life. Imagine if that was your only goal? Every time your refrigerator is full, you're a success. The simplicity of Africa can change your perspective on what's real and what's not - what's important in life.

The thing I love most about Africa are the people. In all fairness I cannot speak for every single African country because I haven't lived in every country in Africa, so I'll speak about the people I know – Zambians. As I mentioned earlier, Zambia is one of those countries that doesn't make the news because it's a peace loving country. Zambia gained its independence from the British in 1964, around the same time that black people in the US were fighting for civil rights. Matter of fact, Zambia's first president Kenneth Kaunda met with Martin Luther King around that time to show his support for the civil rights movement. You can google "Kaunda and MLK," and you'll see images and details of that meeting.

Zambian people or I should say Africans, in general, are a very welcoming people. Sometimes I wonder if this spirit of hospitality is the reason Africans were colonized by Europe. It seems as though Africans are always welcoming people into their homes. Which is mainly a result of custom and tradition.

Growing up I remember once counting twenty-two family members living in our home – a three bedroom home. But that's just how Africans are. A family member or friend can literally show up at your home unannounced expecting a place to stay and food – and they'll get it.

Not in the US though. It doesn't work quite that way here. The 'tradition' here is that there's nothing for free. Even if your own brother or sister asks to come live with you, the expectation is that they pay rent or give you a move-out date you can live with.

Maybe if Africans weren't so hospitable, they might not have been colonized. They might have charged the Europeans 'rent', to remind them that they were just visitors. But I'm sure it wasn't as simple as that.

If you've hung around Africans, then you probably noticed that they take education very seriously. This is something I think Africa does well. Though most African countries are poor, they invest heavily in education. I'm not talking about the type of investment that just throws dollars at a problem, but instead, I'm talking about investment in the idea of education.

Africans will have you pumped to go to school. The popular kids in school were the smart kids. What in America we call nerds, in Africa would be considered the coolest kids in school. If you were good at math, you were a stud. Everyone wanted to be your friend.

Ironically the infrastructure of the schools is a sad situation. Some schools don't even have desks for kids to sit on. They just sit on the floor. The buildings are crumbling. There is no gymnasium in the American sense. Sports is mainly limited to track & field and soccer. On a dusty open area called a "field." Now, of course, this is not the case in all of Africa. I'm simply giving you an account of my experience.

Despite all the lack of material advantages, I would say I received a quality education in Zambia. Which is evident by the fact that I was able to graduate from college in the U.S. Most notable of my education was my secondary school education. What is known here as High School.

I went to an all-boys Catholic High School. It was a prestigious High School by Zambian standards. The prestige didn't come from anything but the fact that kids who graduated from there were considered 'smart kids.' The entrance exam score was slightly higher than other high schools in the area. But what made our school even more prestigious was the fact that we had white men as teachers. Yea, imagine that – just the color of a teacher's skin made all the difference.

Africa, though reluctant to admit it, has a white supremacy problem – and it's not perpetuated by whites. Many black people sincerely believe that Europeans are intellectually superior to Africans. Why the African-American tribe really needs to step in, but I digress…So being taught by a European was an honor of sorts. Crazy, right? Regardless of the racial politics, I'm grateful to those white men for what they did teach me. I can't take anything away from the fact that they did their job. These men had traveled from Ireland to come to this little town in the middle of Africa to teach – much respect. I just don't think they were intellectually superior to the black teachers who also taught me.

I can't wait for the day African-American teacher's travel to Africa to do the same. I think African-Americans have so much knowledge to share with Africans, and so much to gain from that whole experience. I'm sure there's a hand full who are doing just that, but I'm speaking of a larger scale.

Our Headmaster was this huge Irish man who went by the name "Brother Orielly." He was about 6'6" with a big belly, huge calve muscles easily noticeable as he almost always wore shorts. I guess it's because Africa was a little warmer than where he was from. He wore big glasses with thick lenses that almost looked like bifocals.

He beat the crap out of us. We feared that man more than we feared the law. I remember having to report to his office after missing a day of school for being sick, I've never felt so guilty for being sick in my life! I never missed school after that. Sick and all, I was going to go to class. It wasn't uncommon to get slapped or punched at least once a week. We never complained because that was our normal. Besides, the black teachers were just as violent, so we knew it wasn't a race issue; partially why I think Africans are slow to cry foul or complain about anything. It's though abuse is normalized. Getting punched and slapped by teachers isn't something the African-American tribe would stand for. There would be an educational revolution. It's for reasons such as this that I say Africa needs the zero tolerance spirit found in the African-American tribe. That spirit is especially needed when making deals with foreign powers. Especially those who've had a history of exploiting Africa.

All we cared about in high school was getting an education. Our life was all school. Going to an all-boys school made it easy to focus on school work while at school. There were no girls around to distract – until after class.

I was thought of as one of the well-off kids because my parents had a car. Imagine that. Back then cars were a sign of upper class. It really didn't matter what kind of car, as long as you had a car. Which is so ironic because I had no shoes my last two years of high school. I wore what we call "rafters" to school. Which basically looked like a cross between flip flops and sandals. These are sandals designed specifically for water rafting – hence "Rafters". Just to be clear, it wasn't because my parents couldn't afford a pair of shoes, they just couldn't afford to import a pair of shoes. I wore a size 13-14, and we just couldn't find my size anywhere in the country. Something I look back at now and just laugh at the ridiculousness of the entire situation. But that's Zambia. At the time it never bothered me not one bit, because I knew that there were people who had real issues. Walking to school in some rafters was no problem. Although at times I got frustrated when it was hot outside, and I'd be walking through the sand on the way to school, and the hot sand would get stuck in between my toes. It just wasn't a comfortable situation.

I remember sitting in class during lunch break daydreaming of what it would be like to be in America.

Even though I was born in the U.S, my family left when I was only months old. I used to watch all the shows and listen to all the music and just think "Americans are so dope." I literally prayed to one day be able to visit the United States of America. I kept a journal of all my thoughts and prayers. I still have it today. I occasionally glance at it to remind myself of how far I've come. America seems so far away for most Africans. It's as though one is saying they're planning to go to the moon.

My classmates would always tease me when I spoke about America. To them, I sounded like a crazed man planning on building a rocket to go to the moon or something. But I kept on praying, and one day, shortly after I graduated from High School, literally a month after graduation, one of my Dads friends was traveling to the U.S on a business trip. My Dad sold a piece of land he owned for what I know had to have been a complete loss and booked my flight to the US. I still didn't have any shoes, and I didn't have any pocket money. Thankfully my flight had a layover in Johannesburg South Africa.

If you're not familiar with Africa, South Africa is the really nice area of Africa, and Johannesburg is one of its biggest cities. So they had my shoe size. There I met my Dad's older brother, my uncle George. Ever since I can remember this man always seemed to have it together. He met me at the airport with two pairs of shoes and gave me $200 pocket money. For some reason, at that moment, between the one-way ticket my Dad bought, the two pairs of shoes and $200 Uncle George gave me, I just knew I had everything I needed to be successful in life.

I arrived in the U.S January of 1999. I remember that day like it was yesterday. The flight was long, I was tired, I was excited, I was scared. I really didn't know what to expect. I had just turned 17, so I didn't have much life experience anyway. The little I did have was all from Africa.

I arrived at around 10 PM. I remember the plane approaching land, and I looked out the window, all I saw was a sea of lights. "This is it!" I thought to myself - "I'm here, in America."

My anxiety level was high. I was arriving in a foreign land, and I pretty much didn't know anyone except my older brother who I hadn't seen since I was six years old. Even then he was away at boarding school for most of the time. It's fair to say I hardly knew even him at the time.

I was met at the airport by my sister-in-law, I remember thinking to myself "I probably stink...what a terrible way to make a first impression". One thing you have to remember about traveling from Africa is that it typically is a two-day journey – at least coming from Zambia it is.

I remember walking outside the airport and breathing that American air for the first time. It was cold, very cold. As you can imagine, I arrived in the Midwest in the middle of winter.

Approximately two weeks after my arrival I secured a Job at the local fast food restaurant. I was hired to make burgers and such, but I found myself doing a lot of the Janitorial work instead. I didn't think much about it. I was just happy I had a job.

It wasn't until one of the black ladies who worked with me pulled me aside and asked me "why do you let them keep doing you like that?" I didn't know what the heck she was talking about. She then asked me "do you see any of the white kids cleaning the bathroom?"

Then it hit me all at once like a ton of bricks – she was talking about racism. I had never experienced racism before. It was something I learned of at school and from watching movies, but I didn't think it still existed, let alone I would be experiencing it firsthand. I told her the work didn't bother me. I just wanted to do whatever it took to survive. Her reply was "well you can do better than cleaning bathrooms to survive." I don't think she had any idea how those words would impact the rest of my life.

I went home and told my brother about what the lady said and what I was now observing. My brother told me just to brush it off, that they were racist assholes everywhere. See, I was fine cleaning the bathrooms and all as a team player, but I had a problem doing it because I was the 'black' team player.

The next day I frankly asked the manager why I was the only person cleaning the bathrooms. I asked to work the window as the other kids. The manager said it was nothing personal he just wanted someone customers could easily understand on the window. His response hurt me. Of course, it was personal. I was being singled out because of my accent. Either way, it was discriminatory. Until that point, I didn't even think my accent was a problem. I went home that evening feeling less-than.

I humbled myself and continued cleaning the bathrooms for the next couple months, until one day I came into work and there was a swastika with the words "save our precious Aryan race" written on the wall in one of the bathroom stalls.

I hadn't experienced racism before, but I watched enough race-related movies to know exactly what that was. I immediately told the manager. I wasn't going to clean that bathroom with that on the wall. I wasn't going to clean it off the wall either. The manager decided to clean it off the wall himself. I guess probably in a good effort gesture.

Again I went home that evening just astonished that this was really happening to me. This is not the America I was longing for. At that moment I got a glimpse of what the African-American tribe has been dealing with all these years. Fully appreciating the fact that what I experienced was, in fact, nothing compared to what they've been through. But it was enough to make me not want to be there.

I had enough with that fast food joint. I decided to look for another job. I got hired at the local grocery store as a stocker, stocking shelves. I thought I had made it in life. At the time it seemed a lot more prestigious than cleaning bathroom floors. I worked the night shift. During the entire time I didn't have a car. Fortunately I had used that $200 my uncle had given me to buy myself a bicycle. I rode to work every day at 11p at night and rode home at 7 am. The nights and early mornings were very cold, but it didn't stop me from going to work.

Working at the grocery store was good for me. I met a diverse group of fellas – all white though. One stood out the most. His name was Brandon. He was an interesting individual in that he loved all things black. He was the whitest person you'll ever meet, but he was a living encyclopedia of black culture. He looked the part too. It was apparent from his choice in clothing that he identified more with Black culture. He was the first person I met with tattoos. He wore a couple of gold chains. He knew and owned every hip hop album I had ever heard of. He even had underground rap that I didn't even know existed. He had a Tupac CD that at that time had never been released. I distinctively remember thinking "how does this dude have Tupac new music and Tupac is dead?"

We got along really well. I almost believe God had me meet up with him to heal the racist incident episode. To show me that not all white people were racist. Because after working at the fast food restaurant, I was beginning to think that. Many people have no idea how easy it is to create mistrust with minority communities. All it takes is one episode of racism without a satisfactory remedy to fix the wrong, for there to be a lifetime of mistrust. This is partially because of the historic racial injustice of minorities.

I learned a lot from him. He even gave me a ride to the local Best Buy to purchase my first Play Station. At 17, that was a big deal to me. Things were beginning to make sense. I was beginning to appreciate America. Unfortunately, that didn't last long.

The store decided they needed a new night manager. They hired some 'dude' who presented himself as having managed one of the biggest stores of a leading competitor. Frankly, that should've been their first red flag. It made no sense that a manager of a leading competitor would need a position as night manager managing only four stockers.

He was a short white man with jet black hair, a mustache like he just came out the 70's, small beady eyes, with one lazy eye. He didn't say much – to me anyway. For some reason whenever he wanted me to do something he would always relay the task through Brandon. I saw it very odd, but I didn't think too much about it.

One day I came to work. No more than ten minutes after clocking in, a voice came over the intercom, "David report to receiving". Receiving was basically the back of the store at the docking area where we would 'receive' the store products.

I didn't think much about it and walked on back to receiving. I entered the receiving area. The new night manager was standing by one of the forklifts, smoking a cigarette. I stood there looking around for the new shipment, as that was typically why I would be called to Receiving, to unload a truck. Before I could even reconcile the fact that there was no truck, he said "We're letting you go". I just thought he meant for the night. It wasn't unusual to have a slow night and for some of us to be sent home early.

I asked what night I may be able to make up my

hours. He must've thought I was trying to be funny. His next words were a very stern "You're fired!" I asked "why?", "What did I do?" He then said "Just get out!" I went to the staff room to get my coat and gloves and proceeded to walk out of the store. Brandon saw me and followed me outside looking confused. I told him I just got fired. He asked why, and I told him I had no idea. Brandon just shook his head and said, "I'm sorry this is happening to you – this is some fucked up shit". As if knowing something I didn't.

I put on my coat and gloves, hopped on my bicycle and peddled back home. It was cold. It was definitely below freezing. The roads were slick, the pavements were iced out. I remember that bike ride home very vividly. I thought about my family back in Africa. I thought about the friends I left, the life I left. I thought about how everyone was so proud of me because they just knew I was doing 'big things', and here I was, fired. I started to playback the previous week in my mind. I wondered "what did I do wrong?"

I didn't sleep at all that night. I stayed up just thinking. When my brother woke up the next morning, I told him I was fired from my job. He asked why, and I told him I wasn't given any reason, I was just told to "get out". My brother said, "No, they can't just fire you without cause. Go back to the store and ask the store manager why you were fired". So I did just that. I went back to the store that morning. The night manager and night crew had already left for the day.

I walked in the store almost feeling embarrassed to be there. I made my way to the store manager's office. His door was open and he was typing something on his computer. When he saw me, he greeted me very warmly. He was always a nice guy. He reminded me of the preacher Benny Hinn, except he was white with blonde hair. I was taken aback by his very warm reception of me, considering I was just fired. But it wasn't long before I figured out that he had no idea of the incident that happened the night before. I asked him "Sir, I just want to know the reason I've been fired." "Fired?" he said, "by who? Who fired you?" I told him the night manager told me I was fired and told me to get out of the store. The look on his face was authentic confusion. He immediately picked up the intercom and called for his assistant manager to come to the office. When the assistant manager walked into the office, the store manager then asked me to repeat what I had just said. So I did. He then asked the assistant manager if he knew anything about it. The assistant manager said that was news to him. So then the manager said since no one made him or his assistant manager aware of my firing or the justification for it, I was free to return to work that night. I walked out of that office feeling good. I felt as though I had accomplished something. In reality, I guess I did. I spoke up and got my job back. Something I wasn't trained to do in Africa. Africans typically are taught to 'respect' authority figures. Unfortunately, this can sometimes mean just saying "ok" to whatever you're told. Traditionally we aren't taught to challenge authority. Something the African-American tribe does very well.

I went back to work that night. Brandon was happy but surprised to see me. I told him that I spoke to the store manager earlier that morning and he told me I still have a job. I was only half way into telling the story of how the conversation went with the store manager when the night manager walked in the staff room. He said, "What the hell are you doing here?!" I could hear the hatred in his voice. I told him that I spoke to the store manager and he said I could come back to work. He walked up to me, and stood in my face and said, "Get out!"

I tried to plead my case to him, asking him repeatedly what I did wrong. Why was he treating me this way? Again his reply was "Just get out!" So I started to walk out, Brandon followed behind me as though to make sure I was leaving the store. But I knew he was cool, he was just playing the part. When we got to the front doors, Brandon again apologized for the whole situation and advised me to come back the next morning and speak to the store manager.

I returned to the store the next morning. The store manager was surprised to see me again. I told him what transpired the night before. He asked me if I told the night manager that he's the one who instructed me to return to work, I said, "Yes, of course." He was furious. I guess he finally realized that the night manager really didn't have any respect for me, let alone him. He told me not to worry about it that he'd have a conversation with him. I then asked, "So what should I do tonight?" "You know all he's going to do is tell me to get out as soon as he sees me." He then asked me if I was fine with doing different work in the store, away from the night manager's authority. I agreed. I was just happy to have a job. Then he said, "great, we need a night janitor." My feelings immediately became sour. I had seen this game before when I worked at the fast food restaurant. I guess my displeasure with this resolution was so obvious because he immediately clarified by saying, "I promise it will only be temporary until we get to the bottom of what's going on with the night manager." I agreed.

That night I returned to work. I guess this time the day crew communicated with the night crew that I will be returning to work as a janitor. So no one was surprised to see me, but I could sense that the fellas were probably warned not to speak to me. No one would say a word to me, not even Brandon. So I just went about my night, cleaning the men's bathroom first, then the women's bathroom. I went up and down the isles sweeping, mopping and polishing the floors. When it was lunch time (Yes night shift do take 'lunch'), I went to eat my food in the staff breakroom – like I always did. I barely started eating when the rest of the night crew walked in, and following behind them was the night manager. He then asked me to leave to the breakroom. He said, "We're about to have a private meeting, find somewhere else to eat your lunch." Now keep in mind, these are stockers. All they do is take stuff out of boxes and put it on shelves. What 'Private' thing would they possibly be meeting about? What he was doing was so obvious; the other guys on the team couldn't even look me in the eye. They all just held their heads down. As if they were embarrassed for him. I just walked out and went to finish my lunch in the back of the store by the loading docks. When they finished in the breakroom, Brandon came looking for me to tell me I could go back in. But by then my lunch break was over, and I was so turned off at the whole idea of even going to sit in that breakroom, that I wouldn't go back even if I had another hour to spare.

At this point, my mind started to turn. It was becoming clear that the night manager had a problem with me. Just me. There was absolutely no rationale behind his behavior. There was only one logical conclusion. This was textbook racism. My mere presence bothered him. At that moment I noticed the color of my skin. I noticed that everyone who was allowed to sit in that breakroom was white. Again I was in disbelief because this was 1999. These are things I thought only happened in the 60s and before.

See, mainstream America will have you believe that racism is a thing of the past. All the movies about racism are staged in the 60's and before. So even when I was in Africa, I would think to myself "It's not like that anymore." Had I known this was how people were still currently being treated, I would've empathized with the current plight of black America long before. Something all Africans need to be aware of – it's not as rosy as it looks.

The next morning I got a call from the store manager asking me if I came to work the night before. Confused, I said, "Yes, I only left a couple of hours earlier." He then asked why the floors were not clean, "The store is a mess." he said. I was confused because I knew for sure I was under a microscope, so I made sure to go above and beyond in cleaning the store. At this point, I didn't trust anybody. I told him I would be right there to see this for myself. I hopped on my bicycle and peddled as fast as I could down to the store.

When I got there, sure enough, the floors were not clean. The floors were white tile so every mark and blemish would show. There were wheel marks of the little trolleys we would use to bring the product in from the back, up and down the aisles. It was terrible. I was astonished because I would always clean the aisles last - after they had finished stocking the shelves and everything was wheeled to the back. To avoid this very occurrence. Luckily I was confident enough in my work that I asked the manager to review the security footage from the night before. I told him "you will see that I swept, mopped and polished every inch of this store before I left...and I made sure to do the aisles after the stockers were done putting stuff on the shelves." He reviewed the tape. Sure enough, the tape revealed that I cleaned the entire store. But it revealed something even more interesting. It revealed that the night manager waited until I left for the day, and then he pulled a trolley, up and down the aisles. He wasn't putting anything on the shelves or anything like that. He was just blatantly scuffing the floors. The store manager said he would have a discussion with the night manager. I found it odd that he didn't seem surprised or at least apologetic to me. Just about thirty minutes ago he was charging me up about not doing my job. Now he just nonchalantly said, "I'll have a talk with him."

I went home again confused at how things worked in this country. I felt the anger that most African-Americans feel. At this point, I was fully aware that race was a major factor. Even though the store manager was 'nice' enough to give me a job, he clearly didn't care enough to correct the situation otherwise it wouldn't have gone on for as long as it did. It was as though he was just doing enough to keep the peace. I wondered if he would have approached the situation differently if the night manager was black and I was a

17-year-old white kid. Would he let any of this go on?

I dreaded going back to work that evening. The series of events had begun to weigh heavily on me. I felt like it was just me against the world. But I knew I had to go back. My parents didn't make enough money to support me, and my brother barely made enough to support his family, so I knew I had to be strong and just weather the storm.

I ensured I made it to work 30 minutes earlier that night. I wasn't going to give the night manager any reason to justify firing me again.

I walked in and made my way to the customer service counter to clock-in. That's where they kept the sign in book. We would sign our names and the time we arrived and left in as log sheet, then at the end of the shift, the manager on duty would sign the log sheet affirming that all was accurate.

I opened the log sheet; lo and behold there was a swastika, drawn in pencil on the page. My second job in the same town and here's this symbol of hate again. Frankly, I wasn't even surprised. Often when I tell this story, people ask me why I didn't take a picture, contact HR, sue, etc. and my response to that is – keep in mind I was a 17-year-old kid from Africa. I had only been in the US for a couple of months. I didn't know how to 'fight' back. But I was getting a lesson in being black in America very quick. Fighting back is something I would have to learn.

I stood there and stared at that page for a couple of minutes, trying to see if I could figure out who drew it. The only person who arrived earlier than me was the night manager, so I concluded it must've been him.

Brandon was the next person to arrive. I was still staring at the log sheet when he arrived. I slid it over the counter to him. He looked down at it to sign his name, then looked up at me. He was in disbelief; his initial reaction was "Did you draw this?" "Of course not!" I replied. We stood there, just staring at each other for a couple of seconds. Then he asked, "Do you think he did it?" He was referring to the night manager. "Yes, there's no one else here" I replied. "I'm sorry man, I don't know what to say," he said. I told him not to worry that I'd just show it to the store manager in the morning.

I went on cleaning the store, avoiding the night manager at every cost. I just wanted to make it through the night. I kept my mind busy with thoughts about Africa. I thought about my hometown Livingstone. How I missed the simple life. How I missed sitting by the river banks of the Zambezi River. The roaring sound of the Victoria Falls, and the everlasting rainbow. I thought about how I took all of that for granted. I questioned myself "This is what I prayed for? This is the better life in America I longed for?"

Morning arrived, I sat at the front of the store waiting for the store manager to arrive before I signed out. When the manager arrived, I asked if I could have a moment of his time, because I had something important to show him. At this point, the night manager had already left for the day. I grabbed the log sheet and just like a bad joke, the swastika was erased. I had no evidence to show the store manager. I told him what was drawn in the log sheet and he looked at me as though I was crazy. Like I just made it up. At this point, I didn't trust anyone. I had enough of this little

American town. I took all the little money I had saved and booked a flight headed back to Africa. I made sure it was a return ticket though. I just needed a couple of months of that African magic to remind me who I was. I returned to the U.S a couple of months later, but this time to a bigger city with a larger population of African-Americans. I was shocked the first time I saw a black man driving a Corvette. That's just something you never saw in the small town I previously lived in. Seeing that gave me hope in America. That's why to this day I'm a strong advocate for positive images of success. Seeing other people being successful inspires us to do the same.

GREATNESS

One thing all Africans must remember about coming to America is that when you arrive, you arrive "black". You're immediately part of the most marginalized demographic. You will struggle against society, and you will struggle against yourself.

Some people will hate you for no other reason than the fact that you're black. They will work against you. They will try to break your spirit.

This is the life of the African-American tribe. Media doesn't capture half of what goes on in black neighborhoods. Outside looking in, one may assume the African-American tribe is just a whining bunch, and that slavery and discrimination are things of the past. But nothing could be further from the truth. The African-American tribe is still fighting a daily racial battle. Some have gotten so used to it, that they barely notice how they've evolved to cope. They've developed split personalities to survive. Almost every successful African-American I know has two distinct dialects. There's their "white voice" and there's their real voice. The white voice is used in job interviews, business meetings, presentations, etc. whenever the audience isn't black. I wasn't aware that I too had adopted this survival technique until one day one of my mentors mentioned it to me. He said, "Had you never told me you were from Africa, I would've never known – you must've worked really hard to lose your accent." I haven't lost my accent at all. My accent and dialect changes depending on my audience. This is something very normal to us. But when you think of it, you should be able to speak as your authentic self at all times without fear of being perceived inferior in any capacity.

Talk "proper" we're told. Which is code for "sound white." Having an extensive vocabulary and being able to articulate yourself intelligently isn't enough, you must 'sound' a certain way. For example, T.I the rapper is known for having an extensive vocabulary and articulates himself very well, but he'll never be known as talking "proper." Because he still articulates himself as a Blackman. Though I'm sure, he too can talk "proper."

Others fortunately or unfortunately, depending on how you look at it, refuse to have these split 'personalities'. They refuse to have to change who they are in order to get a job or any other opportunity that requires a certain level of whiteness. What can be unfortunate about this, is that sometimes it means being turned down for opportunities. Especially client-facing, white-collar opportunities. But I admire anyone who stays themselves at all times. Anyone who sounds the exact same whether speaking to a black or white audience.

The 'conscious' community comes to mind. Their style in dress and presentation is very similar to Africans living on the continent. They take pride in their heritage and are unapologetically black.

I have nothing but wonderful things to say about the conscious community. They understand more than anyone else the importance of connection with the motherland. They are constantly reminding each other of who they are.

The one thing I would suggest to the conscious community and all in the African-American tribe is not to only look for greatness in the Africa of a thousand years ago. While it is very true that ancient Africa had great civilizations with Kings and Queens who bowed down to no man, we must not forget the greatness of the African-American tribe. I've seen so many people in the conscious community try to skip over their African-American identity and only identify with ancient Africa. They feel as though the American experience speaks only to slavery, bondage, and discrimination. It doesn't sync with the "Kings and Queens" narrative that they wish to perpetuate. But this is where they're wrong.

African-Americans are the greatest African tribe. While many may not see it now, I believe hundreds of years from now when people will speak of African empires, they will speak of the African-American empire.

I'm very proud of Africa's heritage. I too speak with great pride when I speak of empires like those established by rulers like Mansa Musa, or the technological advances of the Egyptians or any other African majesty, but I can't help but wonder, what the hell happened? Who dropped the ball? How did Africa go from being the pioneer in civilization to being the poorest continent in the world?

Yes, we know that the answer has a lot to do with the Europeans, but we must remember that Africa was ahead of the learning curve way before Europe. Europeans had to first catch up before they could overtake. America as we know it, didn't even exist at the time. So why did those great Kings and Queens of Africa allow the continent to fall behind the rest of the world? They had every advantage available to them. They had the education, they had the resources, they had the manpower, they had culture, they had home-court advantage, they had it all. But still, somehow the Europeans managed to convince them that they were inferior, and literally took over the entire continent, drew borders and forced them to learn European languages. To be fair, this wasn't just an African problem, Europeans took over the entire world.

STRONGEST
BLOODLINE

Approximately four to five hundred years ago people were kidnapped from the Africa. These people were then sold as slaves and shipped to the new world. The journey alone was the things of nightmares. Many Africans died along the way. It was hell on earth. Only the strong survived.

I want you to stop and absorb this for a moment – "Only the STRONG made it." Meaning, of the Africans who were kidnapped only the strong were able to endure that journey across the ocean. This is the first bit of evidence of the making of a great African tribe.

When these remaining very strong Africans made it to the new world, they were then sold into slavery. They were tortured. Their lives were living hells. The slave masters did everything they possibly could to break the spirit of those Africans, and many more died. What was left were the very strong.

Stop and absorb that too. We started out with different bloodlines of Africans being kidnapped. Many were lost at sea. While our hearts weep for those lost at sea, we must acknowledge the physical and mental strength of those who made it to the new world. Then, during the first couple years or however long it took to break them in, many more died. So the remaining bloodlines were of those who were even stronger both physically and mentally. The strongest of the strongest.

There's evidence of slave masters selectively breeding these Africans. They literally would look at an Africans physical appearance and abilities and would breed them to make 'better slaves'.

So now you have the selective breeding of the very strongest Africans, whose offspring are now hybrids of Africa's strongest bloodlines.

Slave masters were many things, but they weren't ignorant to the increasing strength of the African-American tribe. They had to have known. They made sure that those offspring forgot who they were. They started programming an inferiority complex into these extraordinary Africans.

They made them feel that their melanin-filled dark skin was ugly. Yet it allowed them to stay hours in the sun. Something the masters couldn't do without health consequences.

They made them feel that their hair was ugly and nappy. Yet when that hair was grown out it was like wool, it provided a natural pillow.

They made them feel that their full lips and shapely African bodies were ugly. Yet the masters lusted after those same bodies.

They made sure they erased Africa from their memory. But see, unbeknownst to them that was an impossible task. The seed of Africa is engraved in every black person, just as the apple tree is in the seed of the apple. Destroying the tree or the fruit doesn't stop the tree from growing again as long as the seed survives. All the seed needs is fertile ground. And that's what America became for these Africans – fertile ground.

Slave masters, had created a hybrid of extremely resilient Africans. Every trial and tribulation only made them stronger. Every time the masters denied these Africans something, it just watered the African seed within. Every time an African was hurt or tortured, that watered the African seed. It wasn't long before there was germination. The African spirit began to show in music, in dance, in arts and crafts of all kinds.

Here were people who had never seen the continent of Africa, yet they sang and danced just as Africans. Their music had a rhythm, uniquely African. Their music would win wars and build bridges.

America couldn't resist the allure of this blackness. It asked for more. It wanted to see them perform their song and dance. It wanted to see them display their hybrid *Africaness* in sports, in film, stage plays, in science and technology.

The more the Africans saw into themselves that which made them who they were, the more the walls began to fall. They created a culture out of nothing. A culture that was birthed of the seed of Africa that was set deep inside every soul.

It is for this reason that the African-American tribe is worthy to be called the greatest African tribe. Unlike the great Kings and Queens of Africa who I dearly respect and many the conscious community celebrate, the African-American tribe started with absolutely nothing. Not their land, not their language, not even their names. But they have built one of the most influential cultures the world has ever seen. It's epic! And it's still in its infancy. You must remember that segregation just ended in the 60's, that's just my parents' generation. So my generation is the first generation to truly be born in a 'free' desegregated world. Can you imagine the achievements of this African-American tribe in the next 100 years? Can you imagine what will be accomplished if they use the full weight of the spear (African continent) behind them? A complete paradigm shift for the black peoples of the world will be an end result.

The African-American tribe fights differently. That's what makes them stronger. Their battles have been won through peaceful protests and intellectual maneuvering. They've beat they're oppressors at their own game on several occasions. Using the same legislative body that enslaved them to free them. This is the bloodline of some of the most resilient Africans, and their strength is in their spirit. Their leaders are patient, slow to anger, calculating and most importantly conscious to the realities of the world. Their ability to forgive is divine. One must remember that the United States has a population of approximately 37 million African-Americans, and it's legal for each one to own a firearm – that's a big army. Yet there's peace. If African-Americans held a grudge or were not forgiving as they are, they would be chaos in the United States. We all saw the havoc in Dallas caused by one person with a gun. But see that's not the African-American way. They fight their battles intellectually. Leveraging their influence in politics, music, sports, science and economics. Since slavery, no matter what gets thrown their way, they've never backed down. They've won every time. And it will keep getting better.

Even though many may not feel it, God has definitely blessed this tribe. He has ordained them with a world stage to lead the struggle for black people all over the world. They are the tip of the African spear.

Most have no idea. Honestly, most I've spoken to feel separate from Africa.

But see, the society which oppressed them has one more trick left up its sleeve. It made sure they continue to hate themselves and their motherland - this is where we find ourselves today.

The media continues to push negative images and narratives about Africa and African beauty. Most African-Americans wouldn't even consider vacationing in Africa. Most prefer European fashion to African fashion. As evident by most social media filtered pictures, some people still think "lighter" is better; Some people still think african hair is ugly. The damage done by centuries of programming is deeply rooted.

But if history is any indicator, it's that African-Americans use negative attacks as a pivot to something greater. I can't wait to see the African fashion revolution. Standards of fashion and beauty will no longer be based on the perceptions of Paris, Milan or London. They will come from the motherland, and the standard will be set by the African-American tribe. Then people will love to wear their natural hair, they will love their dark skin, etc.

THE NEXT 100 YEARS

Wat do you think the plight of the Blackman will be in the next 100 years? Are any of the black leaders in Africa or America seriously planning for the next 100 years?

Think about your descendants for a moment. A hundred years from now you will be someone's ancestor. Seriously ponder that. What legacy will you leave for them? Will they know the same world that you know, where mostly African-American and African are two very different peoples with the only thing shared in common is the color of their skin and some distant ancestor? Or will they inherit a world where "African-American" means the "The greatest African Tribe – the tip of the African spear."

As I mentioned earlier, I've seen firsthand China taking an active interest in Africa. They are surely laying the ground work for the next 50 - 100 years. If in the next 100 years any other foreign power such as China is the biggest player in Africa while African-Americans are still fighting for economic equality in the United States then our generation would have failed.

At some point, Africans and African-Americans need to come to a conscious awareness of mutual self-preservation. I believe that moment is now. There must be round table discussions between leaders in the African-American tribe and the tribes in Africa. Getting to know one another and laying out the foundation for active relationships for the next 100 years.

This alone will fill the cultural identity void which has been present since slavery.

The African-American tribe needs to have a seat at the African table in planning the future of Africa. The irony is that the seat has always been there, available for African-Americans decedents of Africa. Except the British, India, China, etc. have been sitting in it.

So one may think this all sounds good, and all, but how true is it? How practical is it that African-Americans can be fully engaged in Africa? The question I get asked the most is, "Are Africans going to be accepting of us?" The answer is yes and no.

Africans on the continent highly admire the African-American tribe. You can ask any African-American who has visited Africa. They will all tell you the same – they were treated with great respect. However, as is in all societies not everyone you meet will feel the same. We can't plan for the next 100 years if we're going to worry about every single persons feelings. We must simply keep our focus on the big picture.

Matter of fact Africans are a little too accepting of all peoples from all around the world. This has proven to be a good and a bad thing, as some investors do not have the best interests of the African people at heart. Frankly, some think that black people are inferior to them. This is why it's so important to have die hard conscious folks doing business with Africa. Africa needs the type of investor whose guiding principle is making wealth while uplifting the global black community. Blacks all around the world can't fight their way out of being the most marginalized race in the world. They can only strategize their way out of it. This is precisely why the African-American tribe must equally take the lead. The African-American tribe has successfully fought and overcome, without the use of violence. Their spirit and culture is a weapon like no other. Something as simple as their music has penetrated the hardest of hearts - tearing down the walls of racism.

You may be wondering what you can do to initiate a sincere connection with the motherland. The answer is simpler than you think – just REMEMBER who you are. Now you may look at yourself and say something like "I'm from Ohio. I'm not from Africa. That's who I am". Which may be true, but it's only partially true. Your story didn't start with you or your parents or grandparents. You are a product of thousands of years. The blood that runs through your veins has been passed down through the centuries. I had a friend once ask me "Do I even have a drop of this thousand-year-old African blood you keep telling me about left in me?" My reply was "Look at your skin. Is it black? If yes, then yes."

Step one is just get acquainted with Africa. Get a map, learn the geography. Study the different regions and learn about the different people. Both past and present. Most African-Americans I've spoken to know everything about Egypt as if it were the whole of

Africa. While I sincerely understand the grandiosity appeal of ancient Egypt, I'd caution to remind folks that it is a very, very small part of the continent. Africa has five sections to it. There's north, south, east, west and central. Get familiar with all the regions. We should all be able to name every country in Africa by just looking at the map and have a basic understanding of the people in every country.

You'll be amazed to discover the complexity of the continent. The sheer number of languages is mind blowing. There are approximately 3000 languages spoken natively in Africa. They are divided into six major language families; Afroasiatic – North Africa, the Horn of Africa, Austronesian – Madagascar, Indo-European – sections of Southern and Northern Africa, Khoe – Namibia and Botswana, Niger-Congo(Bantu) West Central, Southeast and Southern Africa and lastly Nilo-Saharan Sudan and Chad.

Acquire a general understanding of as many cultures as you can. Find the one that speaks to you. I personally believe as crazy as it sounds that we're guided by our ancestors. They leave us little clues and hints, bread crumbs if you may, of what direction we need to go whenever we seek something. It was the dream about my ancestor that inspired this book. So I sincerely believe that if you just took a moment to learn the different cultures and regions of Africa, you'd find something that will feel familiar to you. Then simply study that particular culture/region in great depth. I suggest this approach because Africa is way too vast to have an in-depth understanding of every culture, region, language, etc. I lived there all my childhood, and I still couldn't tell you all there is to know. But I sure can tell you about Southern Africa and Zambia in particular. I even purchased some land in Zambia. That leads me to the next point – economics.

Just as not everybody is an entrepreneur, not everybody can have a direct economic connection. But for those business savvy individuals - once you have an understanding of the entire continent of Africa, and you've found a region or people that appeal to you, get familiar with the economics of that area. What natural resources do they have? How much does an acre of land cost? What do people there need? What business opportunity might arise for you based on the need?

Now you may be thinking to yourself that purchasing land in Africa is just not for you. You never see yourself living there, nor do you have an interest in living there, and that's ok. Again, you must remember that not everything you do is for you, it's for your descendants. So just because you may not see the value in owning land there today, doesn't mean your grandchildren won't have value for it. Hypothetically speaking, if you could purchase an acre of land for about two thousand dollars, would you do it? Most people get more than that on their tax returns. You may be thinking to yourself "but Africa is so far away, it's just a bad investment". But then you'd be very wrong. Africa is just 16 hours away. You'd travel to Africa on a Monday, spend a couple of days doing your business and be back in time for the weekend. And here's the kicker- Americans are doing it. Just not the AFRICAN-American tribe. When I was in my hometown of Livingstone Zambia, I remember meeting many Americans. Matter of fact one of my best friends growing up was an American from Houston Texas. He literally had blonde hair and blue eyes. His family had moved to Zambia because they were tired of the stress of everyday life in the U.S. His Dad set up a makeshift church at the local school. Not once did I ever meet an African-American though. It's not to say that African-Americans don't travel to Africa, matter of fact I know several who have, but I don't think African-Americans travel to Africa as much as they should, given, it's literally their ancestral homeland. I know many people who take vacations every year, but Africa is never on the list.

In my opinion, the last thing that must be done to defeat the psychological warfare brought about by slavery is for the African-American tribe to take pride in Africa. And I'm not talking about just in words, but in deeds as well.

When the captors began their deprogramming exercise of removing the culture, names, language from the Africans, it was to make the Africans FOREVER their slaves. And in many ways, many are still because they have a Eurocentric world view. They don't see the beauty in Africa; they see beauty in all things European. We need economic emancipation. It means choosing to go on an African Safari over going to Paris, France. Choosing to go chill on a beach in Zanzibar over going to Greece.

Dollars matter, where you choose to spend your dollars matters. We can't continue to be up in arms of the economic conditions of black people around the world, including here in the United States and not even spend our money in those communities.

As long as Africa is 'Poor' the African-American

tribe and black people all around the world will continue being marginalized. We can call ourselves Kings and Queens all day, but as long as the Kingdom is in shambles, no one will respect us. This is why the fate of the African-American tribe is tied directly to Africa.

Imagine for a second, if all the images that came out of Africa whereas those of Dubai. Imagine for a second that the African continent was the wealthiest continent on earth. Do you think the African-American tribe would continue to face the injustice they face in the U.S? I think not.

We need an active 100-year strategy of full engagement with the motherland.

Make friends with Africans that are here in the United States. Every African-American should know at least one African. Get to know them, ask questions. I've heard people say "They (Africans) think they're better than us." Some probably do and some don't. No different from black New Yorkers thinking they're 'better' than a black person from Mississippi. I know many who come here and assimilate becoming part of the African-American tribe. Think about it - you wouldn't travel to Africa to assimilate with a particular African tribe if you thought Africa was beneath you, would you? So could one then make the argument that those African-Americans who can afford to travel to Africa but don't, think they're better than Africans?

Do you see how pointless and unproductive it is to focus on those petty points?

Something that I've noticed that turns people off about the topic of Africa is some believe that means moving to Africa. To that, I say, "be where you're most comfortable". Living in Africa is not for everybody, just like country life is not for everybody. Some people think it's the best thing ever; others couldn't disagree more. Precisely why it's important to visit at least once to know what works for you. Ultimately you want to be where you're able to make the most impact for your life's purpose.

The ideas I'm proposing are not "Let's all pack up and move to Africa." No – matter of fact Hell no! African-American culture is perfectly unique and must continue to flourish in the world's super power. What I'm proposing is that the African-American tribe keep doing what it's been doing, but in addition to that, include Africa to its portfolio.

Oprah and Michael Jackson are the two celebrities that come to mind who have done just that. Oprah built a school in South Africa and occasionally visits. Michael Jackson also had a home in South Africa. Also, I know Will Smith recently visited Zambia, but from what I heard, he was there only for a couple of hours. While I wished he had spent more time, I appreciate the fact that he just made the effort. Zambia's tourism industry benefited greatly from his visit.

LOVE BLACKNESS

I f you take away anything from reading this book it should be this – Find and love your God-given identity. As we grow up we form all sorts of identities depending on our environment. But that which you cannot escape is your identity given to you at birth and before birth.

Sadly there's been a century-long assault on black identity, and as a result, some of us have become victims to an inferiority complex. This inferiority complex is evident in different ways. For some, it means bleaching their skin or changing their hair, eye color, etc. For others, it's trying to over compensate – stating that black people are superior in one way or another compared to other races. If you really love yourself, you should be able to say all the things you love about yourself without comparing yourself to anyone.

I recently asked some friends on Facebook about what they loved about being black, and almost all the responses were physical. I have to remind people that being "black" is not just a skin color. It also encompasses our mental and spiritual state.

When people ask me what I love about being black, my first response is, **"I love our story"**.

Your story is the most important thing about you. Why is this story important? It puts into perspective who you are.

For example, if you were dating, and two people approached you, one spent the last five years slaving at a job he/she hated, but they did it anyway because they had a vision to one day purchase a home, but currently had very little to show for it. And the other never worked a day in their life but has a brand new home, purchased with stolen identity. If you didn't know the background stories, you would think the one who already has a home is more successful. When in actuality you're comparing an honest man to a thief. This, is why when asked what I love the most about being black, I say "our story." Africa may be poor, and we may not be where we want to be, but we didn't take any shortcuts, we didn't exploit, cheat or rob anyone along the way. We've been cheated many times, but somehow we just turn the other cheek and hold no grudges. Feel proud about that. Your ancestors were dignified men and women. You come from a long line of honest, humble people.

Next, I love our spiritual connection. We're not an intrinsically material people. Africans have always had a connection to the spiritual world. Material possessions came secondary to spirituality. This is in part the reason it was so easy for the Europeans and Arabs to convince Africans to convert to Christianity or Islam. It's a shame that Africa's resources were plundered in the process though.

I love our love for family. Africans are a collective society, which means the needs of the family outweigh the needs of the individual. We look out for one another. We don't have families; we have clans, villages. Why do I call the African-American collective a tribe? It's one big family. We need to start treating each other as such.

I love our love for music. Africans have been gifted with music. Music to us is an intricate part of life. Music ranks high, right up there with food, water, and air, as one of the most important things in life.

I love our desire to learn. One of the earliest universities in the world was located in Timbuktu, Africa. We're not new to the concept of education. Learning is part of our internal fabric.

I love our love for fashion. Look up the oldest pictures of Africans you can possibly find, and I can almost guarantee that there's something stylish about them. Either some tattoo, jewelry or fashion accessory. We're not new to the fashion. Humor yourself and google "African" and all you'll see are pictures, full of beautiful fabrics, color, and jewelry.

Lastly, I love everything physical about ourselves. I'm not going to name off each feature, and why it's so awesome. Simply because I don't want to draw a comparison with those that may not have the same features, so all I'm going to say is - love yourself – in the whole scope of human physiology, you're pretty impressive.

REMEMBER WHO
YOU ARE

I n conclusion this book has been about remembering who you are. Remembering who WE are as a people. All our accomplishments and all we're yet to accomplish.

I began the book with an example of a fictional character who knew exactly who she was – Khaleesi, on Game of Thrones. Fittingly, her story follows her rise from a 'nobody' to becoming queen of several nations, all because she never forgot who she was. She was always a queen; even when she had nothing. Every time she overcame an obstacle or achieved a goal, she would add another title to her name.

In the same fashion, when you tell yourself or tell others exactly who you are, make sure you mention "…Child of Africa, Breaker of Chains, The Unbroken, Master of Science, God (ess) of Music and Fashion, The Greatest African Tribe.

NOTES

NOTES

NOTES

The End

Made in the USA
Middletown, DE
06 December 2018